Cedomilj Mijatovic

Constantine

The Conquest of Constantinople by the Turks

Cedomilj Mijatovic

Constantine

The Conquest of Constantinople by the Turks

ISBN/EAN: 9783337292485

Printed in Europe, USA, Canada, Australia, Japan

Cover: Foto ©ninafisch / pixelio.de

More available books at **www.hansebooks.com**

CONSTANTINE

The Last Emperor of the Greeks

OR

THE CONQUEST OF CONSTANTINOPLE BY THE TURKS

(A.D. 1453)

AFTER THE LATEST HISTORICAL RESEARCHES

BY

CHEDOMIL MIJATOVICH

FORMERLY SERVIAN MINISTER AT THE COURT OF ST JAMES

London
SAMPSON LOW, MARSTON & COMPANY
Limited
St Dunstan's House
FETTER LANE, FLEET STREET, E.C.
1892

[*All rights reserved*]

WITH PROFOUND ADMIRATION OF THE HEROISM DISPLAYED

BY

CONSTANTINE PALÆOLOGOS

Dedicated

MOST RESPECTFULLY AND BY SPECIAL PERMISSION

TO HIS ROYAL HIGHNESS

PRINCE CONSTANTINE

DUKE OF SPARTA

HEIR TO THE THRONE OF GREECE

PREFACE.

THE German Emperor Frederic III. in a letter written June 1453 to Pope Nicholas V., lamenting greatly the catastrophe on the Bosphorus, calls Constantinople "*the capital of the Eastern Empire, the head of Greece, the home of arts and literature*" ("Orientalis imperii sedem, Græciæ caput .... veluti domicilium litterarum artiumque").[1] And indeed, from the time of Constantine the Great to the time when the dawn of Renaissance aroused Italy to her noble task, Constantinople was the capital of Christian civilization. Its place in the history of the world has been always a most remarkable one,—Rome being the only city which can successfully bear comparison with it.

When in 1453 it passed into the hands of Mohammed

---

[1] The whole text of Frederic's long and interesting letter in Raynaldi, *Annales Ecclesiastici*, vol. xviii., Coloniæ Agr. 1694, p. 408.

El-Fathi its possession consolidated at once the new Mohammedan Empire, and enabled the Sultans of the Ottoman Turks to extend their sway up to the blue Carpathians in the north-west and to the Gulf of Persia in the south-east. There seems almost a miraculous telepathic influence in that place, an influence which inspires its occupants, as long as they possess some power, with an irresistible ambition to rule over three worlds, and which enables old and exhausted Empires to live longer than the most flattering prophecies ever thought probable or possible.

There are theories which assert that the possession of Constantinople enervates, disorganizes, and in the end kills. So far as I have been able to read history, I have found that he who takes Constantinople, once securely seated on the Bosphorus, unavoidably feels that his power is strengthened for a higher task, that his political horizon has widened to the misty limits of an Universal Empire, and that it is the manifest destiny of Constantinople to be the capital, if not of an universal, then at least of a great Empire, stretching over Europe, Asia, and Africa. And I would even say that it seems to me that neither the Byzantine nor the Ottoman Empires could have withstood so long the consequences of disorganization if their capital had not been Constantinople.

It is somewhat singular that, notwithstanding the undoubted interest which European nations in general, and the British in particular, feel in everything connected with Constantinople, the great catastrophe of 1453, so tragic in its incidents and so terrible in its consequences, has never yet been fully and thoroughly worked out and placed before the readers of history. I do not flatter myself for a moment that I shall be able to do what others have not done. I wish only to state, as an undeniable fact, that up to the present no work on, and no description of, the conquest of Constantinople has used all the materials which exist in our time.

Gibbon wrote his incomparably graphic description (vol. iii. 702–730), using only the Byzantine historians, Phrantzes, Ducas, and Chalcochondylas, and the letter addressed to the Pope Nicholas V. by the Archbishop Leonardo of Chios.

The famous historian of the Ottoman Empire, Joseph von Hammer, looked to the same sources of information, adding some scanty notes from the Turkish historian Sa'ad-ud-din.

J. W. Zinkeisen, in his *Geschichte des Osmanischen Reiches* (i. 833–866) was able to use letters and reports found in the Vatican Library.

Mr S. Martin and Mr Brosset (*Histoire du Bas Empire*, par Lebeau) improved Mr Lebeau's description by details found in the poem of the Armenian Abraham, and in the so-called "Grusian Chronicle."

The Russian historian Mr Stassulevich, in his work *Ossada i vzyatiye Vizantii Turkami* (St Petersburg, 1854), used only the old Byzantine sources and the chronicle of Sa'ad-ud-din.

Mr Sreznyevsky published in 1855 an old Slavonic chronicle, *Povyest o Tzaregradye*, accompanying it with notes from Byzantine sources and from Leonardo of Chios.

Dr A. D. Mordtmann has given us one of the most interesting descriptions in his *Belagerung und Eroberung Constantinopels durch die Türken im Jahre 1453, nach Original-Quellen bearbeitet* (Stuttgart, 1858), using largely the Journal of Nicolo Barbaro.

Professor Dr Y. U. Krause (*Die Eroberungen von Constantinopel in XIII und XV Jahrhundert, nach Byzantinischen, Frankischen und Türkischen Quellen und*

Berichten, Halle, 1870) drew principally from Byzantine authors, reprinting some portions from Sa'ad-uddin, and taking some incidents from the poem of a Greek eye-witness.

Rev. W. J. Broadribb and Mr Walter Besant (*Constantinople, a Sketch of its History from its Foundation to its Conquest by the Turks in* 1453, London, 1879) followed Mordtmann and Krause, but consulted also independently Byzantine authors, and added some interesting information on the condition of Constantinople, given by the French knight Bertrandon de la Brocquière.

The latest monograph that appeared in Western literature is that one written by Mr E. A. Vlasto (*Les derniers jours de Constantinople*, Paris, 1883). The author has mainly reproduced the general results of the researches of modern Greek historians, and especially those of Mr C. Paparrigopoulo; but his able work leaves you the impression of being more a political dissertation than a historical picture of the catastrophe.

It is rather singular that there should not exist a single monograph on the Conquest of Constantinople by the Turks in English, though as early as in

1675 a tragedy entitled *The Siege of Constantinople* was published in London.

I believe that, by carefully comparing the statements of eye-witnesses and contemporaries of the siege, as well as the letters and documents of the time, preserved in the Italian and other archives—it would be possible to give a tolerably complete and reliable account of one of the most stirring and important events of history. In the chapters which follow I shall give the result of my attempt in that direction.

I venture to hope that at the present time, when an uncomfortable feeling that Constantinople may soon again change masters pervades the world, political as well as military men will find this little work worthy of perusal, at least for the sake of the great subject of which it treats.

CHEDOMIL MIJATOVICH.

KENSINGTON, *January* 1892.

CONTENTS.

CHAPTER I.
Moral Causes of the Rapid Rise of the Ottoman and the Fall of the Byzantine Empires . . . 1

CHAPTER II.
The Superior Military Organization of the Turks . 27

CHAPTER III.
On the Eve of the Fall . 44

CHAPTER IV.
Diplomatic Negotiations and Preparations for War 76

CHAPTER V.
Military Arrangements of the Besiegers and of the Besieged 131

CHAPTER VI.
The Diaries of the Siege . . . 150

CHAPTER VII.

The Last Days . . 187

CHAPTER VIII.

The Last Night . 206

CHAPTER IX.

The Last Hours . 219

APPENDIX.

The Bibliography . . 231

ILLUSTRATIONS.

1. Constantine, the last Emperor of the Greeks . 85
2. Mohammed II., the Conqueror of Constantinople 90
3. The Fort Rumili-Hissar . . 112
4. The First Naval Battle of the Turks . 158
5. The Turks in St Sophia 222

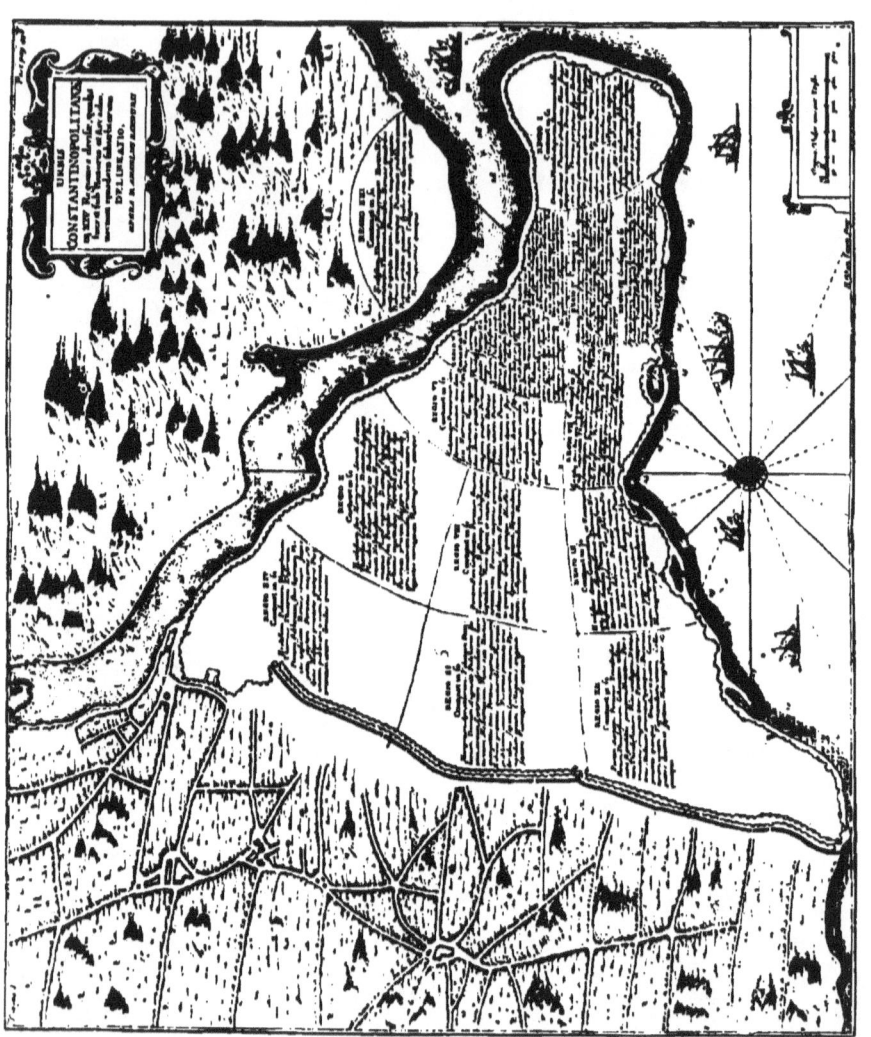

BUONDELMONTI'S PLAN OF CONSTANTINOPLE FROM THE IMPERIUM ORIENTALE, 1711.

CHAPTER I.

MORAL CAUSES OF THE RAPID RISE OF THE OTTOMAN AND THE FALL OF THE BYZANTINE EMPIRES.

1. *Islam and Byzantinism.*

1. IN the one hundred years from the middle of the fourteenth to the middle of the fifteenth century (1365–1465) events deeply tragical in their character and of great historical importance occurred on the Balkanic Peninsula.

An entire change of social and political conditions was accomplished amidst terrible convulsions, accompanied by fearful bloodshed and unspeakable suffering. A foreign race, a strange religion, and a low culture took possession of the beautiful regions between three seas, where once a highly gifted and comparatively cultured people formed and kept up independent states.

It is one of the most interesting unsolved problems of history how an uncivilized and by no means numerous tribe so speedily succeeded in destroying three Christian kingdoms of a higher degree of culture, and in building up in their stead an extensive, powerful, and enduring Empire.

The great fact, however, stands out prominently, assuming the dignity of a general law, that *organization of forces*, although these may be small in themselves and low in their inspirations, *is always victorious over disorganized forces*, even though the latter be great, and superior in their individual character.

2. The Turks were not destitute of certain virtues and natural gifts when they left the Turcoman steppes and came to Armenia to guard the eastern frontier of the Seldjuk Sultans; but after their acceptance of Islam their national character went through an evolutionary change. The sparks of fire thrown out of the volcanic soul of the great Prophet of Arabia inflamed the susceptible sons of the Asiatic deserts, and the metal of their original character was molten and crystallized into a new form of national individuality, capable of the accomplishment of the great, and even more terrible than great, task assigned to them by Providence. As an irresistible avalanche, they moved westward, breaking down and burying all political and national organizations whose elasticity had been weakened and whose strength had been undermined by ages of abuse and mismanagement.

Islam not only impressed upon Ertoghrul and his

followers the duty of being upright before God, truthful and charitable amongst men, but gave them political ideas, transforming a tribe of nomads into a body of warriors and statesmen, capable of creating, maintaining, and developing a great empire. Islam filled them to overflowing with genuine religious enthusiasm, and with the belief that to serve God meant to subdue the Infidels, and conquer the world. This, their central idea, was a bond of unity, giving them political purpose and organization. Their faith immeasurably increased the forces inherent in an energetic, hardy, and astute race.

3. But all the energy of a youthful and hardy race, all their admirable organization, and the high spirit with which Islam inspired the Turks, would not of themselves explain the swift extension of the Turkish rule in Europe. Had the valiant and enthusiastic followers of Mohammed encountered even one really strong, healthy, and well-organized State on this side of the Hellespont, it is doubtful whether the pages of history would have recorded the wonderful growth of the Ottoman Empire. To decipher the secret of that rapid triumphant march we must read the record not only in the lurid glare which conquering Islam gives, but also by the pallid light shed by dying Byzantinism.

It is not easy to describe in a few words what Byzantinism was. It seems as though historic Providence had desired to see the harvest which could be raised, if the seed of Christian civilization should be sown on the peninsula between Asia and Europe, watered by Western rains and warmed by Eastern suns, on fields abandoned by Hellenic culture and somewhat ploughed by Roman institutions. It might have been hoped that the Divine idea of brotherhood would unite the warm heart of New Rome and the practical reason of Old Rome into an admirable harmony, capable of lifting humanity to heights as yet unattained.

But the experiment was not a success. The great forces, from the combination of which so much might have been expected, proved barren. From the spirit of the East some colours and some forms were accepted, but little of its depth, and warmth, and inherent nobility. From Eastern Philosophy only a few more or less nebulous ideas of mysticism were retained; and what of good was borrowed from Roman institutions took no real root, because Roman institutions presuppose a consciousness of responsibility, and also initiative and civic sentiment. What took the deepest root were the forms and spirit of autocratic government from the worst times of the Roman Imperialism, which made the existence of individual liberty impossible. The Christian religion was too abstract, too sublime to be fully understood; it was pushed backward to let the Church come forward.

And the Church identified itself very speedily with the compactly-organized body of ignorant, superstitious, selfish and ambitious monks and priests, who exalted the position of the Emperor only to use him as their servant, and who made practical Christianity mean adoration of old bones, rags, and mummies, and the buying and selling of prayers for the repose of the souls of the dead. The people, having been led astray from the pure source of evangelical truth, found new power nowhere, nor a new idea capable of moving them to great and glorious action. The Emperors and the Church hierarchy became allies, and remained so to the last.

Before the blast of that powerful alliance the sparks of individual liberty were quickly extinguished. Revolutions only made matters worse, because they gave occasions for the display of brutal force, cruelty, servility, and treason, and ended by strengthening the autocracy. Every generous instinct was crushed out to recompense base selfishness and vile ingratitude. The nation became an inert mass, without initiative and without will. Before the Emperor and the Church prelates it grovelled in the dust; behind them it rose up to spit at them and shake its fist. Tyranny and exploitation above, hatred and cowardice beneath; cruelty often, hypocrisy always and everywhere, in the upper and lower strata. Outward polish and dexterity replaced true culture; phraseology hid lack of ideas.

Both political and social bodies were alike rotten; the spirit of the nation was languid, devoid of all elasticity. Selfishness placed itself on the throne of public interest, and tried to cover its hideousness with the mantle of false patriotism.

This political and social system, in which straightforwardness and manliness were replaced by astuteness, hypocrisy, and cowardice, while, however, there still lingered love for fine forms and refined manners,—this system, in which the State generally appears in the ecclesiastical garb, bore the name of *Byzantinism*.

4. It was inevitable that some Byzantinism should enter into the political and social organism of the Slavonic nations of the Balkan Peninsula. Practically they went to the Byzantine Greeks to learn political and social wisdom, just as they went to Constantinople for their religion. It was a slow and exhausting process by which Byzantine notions displaced Slavonic traditions among the Serbians and Bulgarians. And this struggle, not unnaturally, contributed to weaken the Slavonic kingdoms. It was in its own way preparing the paths for the Turkish invasion.

It is especially noteworthy that we find so many Serbian and Bulgarian malcontents in the camp and at the Court of the Ottoman Sultans. The social and political conditions of those Slavonic kingdoms of the Balkans were highly unsatisfactory. The nobles

(Vlastela) were haughty and exclusive. They jealously watched the kings, and resented bitterly every attempt at reform. They were hard and exacting masters to the tillers of the soil settled on their estates, who had to do much personal service, and to give a large part of the produce of their labour. The power, centred in the kings, was not strong enough to prevent all sorts of abuse on the part of the privileged class. Emperor Stephan Dushan essayed to fix by legal enactments the duties of the peasants towards their feudal lords. At the Parliament held in 1349 at Scopia he obtained the consent of his noblemen and high ecclesiastic dignitaries to such a law, and a certain protection of the central power was extended to the peasantry. But after the death of this most remarkable man in Serbian history, the authority of the Central Government was shattered, and if the landlord acted unjustly there were none to protect the injured tenant. In Bosnia, even so late as in the beginning of the fifteenth century, some of the landlords regularly exported their peasants and sold them as slaves!

5. The consequence of such a state of things was that the peasantry, the great bulk of the population, hating their unjust and exacting masters, became more and more indifferent to the fate of the country. The first Sultans, on their part, systematically, from the very beginning of their settlement in Europe, protected and ostentatiously aimed at satisfying the

peasantry, never neglecting any occasion publicly to manifest their desire to do justice to the poor. At the same time they ruthlessly exterminated the national aristocracy. Therefore when the horrors of the invasion had passed away, the peasantry quickly reconciled themselves to the Turkish rule, which in some respects seems to have brought them a change for the better. Numerous proofs might be adduced for this assertion, however paradoxical it may appear to-day.

In a letter written by Stephan, the last king of Bosnia, in 1463 to Pope Pius II., we find these remarkable words: "*The Turks promise to all who side with them freedom, and the rough mind of the peasants* (RUSTICORUM RUDE INGENIUM) *does not understand the artfulness of such a promise, and believes that such freedom will last for ever; and so it may happen that the misguided common people may turn away from me, unless they see that I am supported by you.*"[1] And when Sultan Mohammed II., the conqueror of Constantinople, invaded Bosnia in 1464, the peasantry would not move against him, saying, "*It is not* OUR *business to defend the king; let the nobles do it!*"[2]

There still exists a letter reporting a conversation between the envoy of the Duke of Milan and King

---

[1] *Pii Secundi P. M. Commentarii Rerum Memorabilium, quae temporibus suis contingerunt*, a R. D. Joanne Gobellino, &c., Romæ, 1584, p. 548.

[2] *Ibid.*

Alfonso of Naples, in December 1455, in which it is said that the Albanian peasantry preferred the rule of the Turks to that of their own nobles! King Alfonso was anxious lest the Albanians should abandon Scanderbegh, and surrender again to the Turks, because "*li homeni de quello paese sono molto affeti al Turcho*, EL QUALE GLI FA UNA BONA E HUMANA SIGNORIA!" These are the words of the king himself![1]

6. The Church in Bulgaria and Serbia, in its material relations with the people, was only another form of aristocracy: it demanded labour, service, and a part of the produce of the land. The monks formed a privileged caste, and did not pay taxes to the State, nor did they share any public burden. Their numbers were continually increasing. The thousands of churches and cloisters built by pious kings, queens, and nobles, were not able to contain them. They were living in towns and villages and in private houses, constantly exposed, and frequently succumbing, to worldly temptations. Very few of them were saints, and the majority managed to forfeit the respect of the people, not only for themselves but for the Church. The great Reformer and Lawgiver, Stephan Dushan, by law forbade monks and nuns to live otherwise than cloistered; but the monks proved

[1] Letter of Albricus Maletta, dated "8th Decemb. 1455 ex Neapol.," in Makusheff, *Italianskie Archivi*, p. 97.

stronger than the mighty Tzar. The mass of the people believed in the miraculous powers of relics, but did not like the monks.

7. This dislike explains to some extent the rapid spread of the religious sect of the Bogumils or Partharenes, especially in Bulgaria and Bosnia. The Orthodox Church fiercely opposed these first rude Protestants of Europe. The history of the religious wars which raged in the Balkan Peninsula through two centuries (1250–1450) has not yet been written; but some of the results of that struggle were evident in the deterioration of the religious life, and in the weakening of the political organization of the Bulgarian, Serbian, and Bosnian kingdoms. In Albania, where the conflict between the Orthodox and the Catholic clergy raged most fiercely, and in Bosnia, where the struggle between the Orthodox Church and the Partharenes lasted longest, Islam speedily found converts.

It is characteristic of the dispositions of the people at this period (1360–1460) that the Calabrian monk Barlaam found warm supporters among the Greeks of Constantinople itself, when he denounced the ignorance and indolence of the monks of the "Holy Mountain Athos." Still more characteristic that Gemistos Plethon, the personal friend of the Emperor John Palæologus, one of the great theological and philosophical lights among the Greeks at the Council of

Florence, thought it necessary *to frame a new religion!* He was certainly not the only man whom Christianity, as it was represented by the Orthodox Church of his time, did not satisfy.

8. In addition to the circumstances of the social and religious life, there were some other influences at work to disorganize the vital forces of the Christian States.

There were almost always several pretenders to the imperial throne in Constantinople and the royal thrones in Bulgaria, Serbia, and Bosnia, who hoped by Turkish help to satisfy their own ambition. Naturally, these claimants were ever hospitably welcomed by the Sultans. Again and again gifted Serbians, or Bulgarians, or Greeks, who in their own country could not rise from the position in which they were born, found an open way to wealth, honour, and power, a path to the saddle of a Beyler Bey (Commander-in-Chief), or to the carpet of a Vizier, and perhaps to the golden cage of one of the daughters · or sisters of the Sultan himself! It seems a paradox to say that the Turks opened new horizons to the people of the Balkan Peninsula. Yet their political system, a combination of absolute despotism with the very broadest democracy, had much in it that was novel and acceptable. To the notions of an average Greek, and especially to the notions of an average Serbian or Bulgarian, that system was not more unnatural or more disagreeable than the feudal system which secured all the good things of the world only to the nobles and the priests.

The presence of Christian malcontents, refugees, pretenders, and adventurers in the Turkish camp and at the Sultan's "Porte," materially aided Turkish policy and Turkish arms to progress from victory to victory. Without them the Turkish Viziers and generals could hardly have obtained that minute and exact knowledge of men and circumstances in Christian countries, which so often astonished their contemporaries. Thus the Porte became promptly informed of the plans of the Christian kings, and was enabled to counteract them. Indeed, the leadership of the new Empire speedily passed into the hands of Christian renegades, and almost all the great statesmen and generals of the Sultans at this period were of Greek, Bulgarian, or Serbian origin.

9. The last-mentioned circumstance constitutes one of the most tragic characteristics of the history of the Balkan nations. Its sadness is deepened by the fatal entanglement of the Christian nations of the Peninsula, who were skilfully compelled to annihilate each other in furtherance of Turkish aggrandisement. In the Turkish army which destroyed the Serbian kingdom on the field of Kossovo (1389), there were numbers of Greek, Bulgarian, and Serbian warriors. Among others, Despot Constantine Dragash (the maternal grandfather of the

last Emperor of the Greeks), followed Sultan Murad I. with a contingent of auxiliary troops. When in the battle near Nicopolis in 1396, the French knights, aided by the Polish and Hungarian cavalry, routed the Janissaries of Bayazed Ildirim, the Sultan's reserve, consisting of several thousands of Serbian Cuirassiers, under the command of Prince Stephan Lazarevich, came rushing down to snatch the victory from the Christians.

The Turks gave proof of their great astuteness, at this early stage of their history, by their using chiefly Christian money and Christian arms to subdue, and afterwards to destroy, the Christian States of the Balkan. It was a general rule of their policy not to occupy at once the country of the defeated Christian Prince, but to impose a heavy tribute in money, and to exact that a contingent of his best soldiers should be regularly provided to fight against the Sultan's enemies, even if the latter were friendly Christian neighbours of the vassal Prince.

10. King Marko (the hero of so many Serbian and Bulgarian national songs) has illustrated well the feeling with which comparatively cultured Christian knights fought in the ranks of the Turkish army. At the commencement of the great battle at Rovine between the Turks and the Vallachs (1394), King Marko turned to his relative, Despot Constantine Dragash, and said: "*I pray God to give victory to the Christians, though I pay for it with my own life!*"

These historic words[1] were only an echo of the pain which many a Christian knight endured when, in the monstrously anomalous position, he had to draw his sword for the Mohammedan Turks against brethren of his own faith. But that anomaly was only one of the bitter, yet inevitable, fruits of Byzantinism.

2. East and West.

1. Byzantinism prepared the way for the Turkish invasion. It enfeebled the Balkan nations, destroyed their mental elasticity, and engendered a selfishness, which ripened into all sorts of wickedness.

Byzantinism on one side and the youthful energy of a religiously disposed tribe of born warriors on the other explain much, but do not explain all; the relations of the Byzantine Empire with the West of Europe must also be considered.

When the Eastern and Western Churches separated (A.D. 1053), they did not part with sorrowing hearts, but with mutual anger and great bitterness. Yet the separation of the Churches was not the beginning of the estrangement; it was rather the result of deeper

---

[1] They are quoted by the Serbian court historian, Constantin the Philosopher, in his *Life of the Despot Stephan the Tall*, written about A.D. 1427, printed in the *Glasnik*, the Journal of the Serbian Learned Society, vol. xxxiii.

under-lying differences of sentiments and opinions. Old Rome and New Rome were not of the same temper, nor of similar nerve and fibre. Separation only deepened their mutual aversion. The priests and monks had done their best to concentrate the latent antipathies and to set them ablaze. The people, when they kissed the hands of their priests, seemed to have received from these, who should have been preachers of peace and charity, only new incentives to hatred and intolerance.

The source of bitterness, opened by ecclesiastical hands even at the foot of the Altar, grew to be a deep river, running in the channels digged by political events.

2. The Normans occupying the south of Italy found it easy to cross over to Albania, a province of the Byzantine Empire. With the benediction of Pope Gregory VII., Robert Guiscar, "Duke by the grace of God and St Peter," besieged Durazzo (Dyrachium) in 1081. This strong place on the Albanian coast of the Adriatic was the key of the famous old Roman road *Via Egnatia*, which, crossing Albania and Macedonia diagonally, led to Salonica, joining there another military road to Constantinople. It might almost be said that Durazzo was the western gate of the Byzantine Empire.

It is worthy of note that even at the occasion of this first attempt by a foreign power to obtain a firm footing in the Balkanic Peninsula, antagonistic interests came into play. While Robert Guiscar and Pope Gregory combined to effect the conquest of the Byzantine Empire, Venice sent her fleet to assist the Emperor in repulsing their attack. And though the Normans defeated the Byzantine army, took Durazzo, and conquered a number of towns and castles in Epirus and Thessaly, yet in the end they had to relinquish their conquests because the German Emperor, Henry IV., invaded Italy.

But the Normans returned to the charge. For nearly a century the Greek Empire had to defend itself against their attacks. Guiscar's expedition was followed by that of Bohemund (A.D. 1107), of King Roger (in 1146), and the great invasion of Tancred (1185). The latter not only took Durazzo and Salonica, but marched into Thracia on his way to Constantinople.

3. The Norman successes had indirectly important results. They helped to destroy the prestige of the Byzantine arms in the eyes of the Serbians, Bulgarians, and Albanians. They shook the weakened Empire, and started its slow dismemberment. They demonstrated to Western Catholic Europe that the conquest of the Eastern Empire was not impossible. And this demonstration fired the ambition of the Popes to convert the East, by arms if not by arguments, and to compel it to bow to Rome. It is significant that this

very Pope Gregory, in a letter written in 1073 to Ebouly de Rossi, declared "*that it is far better for a country to remain under the rule of Islam, than be governed by Christians who refuse to acknowledge the rights of the Catholic Church.*"[1] The Orient's answer to this we shall learn from the excited Greeks in the days preceding the great catastrophe.

The lesson which the Norman warfare in Albania and Epirus taught began to bear fruit already towards the end of the twelfth century. The Serbians, vassals of the Greek emperors, sought alliances in the West, with the evident intention of establishing a strong and independent State of their own on the ruins of the Byzantine Empire. Stephan Nemanya, the founder of the Serbian royal dynasty of Nemanyich, endeavoured by special embassies to approach the German Emperor Frederick Barbarossa, and in 1189 received him and his Crusaders with great hospitality at Nish. The *Memoirs* of Ansbertus, the Emperor's secretary, state that the Serbian Prince urged the Emperor to make himself master of the Byzantine Empire, promising him assistance. From another chronicler in the suite of Barbarossa we learn that Nemanya made these proposals in the names of his allies, Peter and Ivan Assen, the chiefs of the Bulgarian nation, as well as in his own name. Frederic was not prepared to

[1] Taffel, *Regest. Pontific.*, No. 3542 ; Gfrœrer, *Byzantinische Geschichten*, ii. 459.

enter into the vast projects of the Serbian ruler. Notwithstanding this, they parted as sincere friends. Ansbertus never mentions Nemanya without adding, "our friend, the great Count of Serbia."[1]

4. The passing of the great and generally undisciplined armies of the Crusaders through Byzantine countries did not improve old feelings or remove old prejudices. On the contrary, it enabled the Western warriors (or, as the Greeks called them, "the Latins") to perceive at once the weakness of the Empire and the unfriendliness of the people. On the other hand, the roughness and rudeness of the Crusaders confirmed the contempt which the Greeks felt for such "Western barbarians."

The bitterness of the Greeks was naturally largely increased by the sudden appearance of the Crusaders under the walls of Constantinople, and by their subsequent conquest of that capital (A.D. 1204). For fifty-seven years (1204–1261) the Latins retained possession of Constantinople and the best European provinces of the Empire. For fifty-seven years the Catholic priests read masses at the altar of St Sophia, to the inexpressible sorrow and humiliation of the patriotic and bigoted orthodox Greeks. During these long, dark years the Greeks, especially the more narrow-minded populace of the capital, were storing up hatred of the Latins, which, even two hundred years later,

[1] Ansbertus in *Fontes Rerum Austriacum*, vol. v. 1-90.

prevented them finding anything more bitter to endure.

Michael Palæologus succeeded in 1261 in driving out the Latins from Constantinople. But he was unable to reconquer the islands, the fortified towns in Thessaly and Morea. Instead of despots and princes bearing the names of the old Greek families, we find a *Guy de la Tremouille*, Baron de Chilandritza, a *Guillaume de la Roche*, Duc d'Athènes, a *Nicholas de Saint-Omer*, Seigneur de Thèbes, *Richard Comte de Cephalonie, Guillaume Allman Baron de Patras, Villain d'Aunoy Baron d'Arcadie, Bertrand de Baux*, " Mareschalcus Achaiae," &c. &c. This combination of French names and feudal titles with the classical names of Athens, Patras, Thebes, Arcadia, Achaia, &c., sounds even in our day strange and almost grotesque. But it must have inspired the patriotic Greeks of those days with frantic hatred and despair. And the highest, the most cultured class in Constantinople, those who under the new dynasty of Palæologus ruled the Empire, could not but feel great humiliation at the thought of the French baronies in the classical territories of the Peloponnesus. Nor could the Greeks be without anxiety whilst the energetic and clever Anjous, the French dynasty of the kingdom of Naples and Sicily, were asserting their pretensions to the Imperial throne of Constantinople. Catherine de Valois, the wife of Philip II. of Anjou, bore proudly the titles of "*Empress of Constantinople, Despotissa of Romania, Duchess of Durazzo, Princess of Achaia,*" &c. &c.

5. The diplomatic and military preparations of Charles I. to reconquer the Byzantiue Empire, which Baldwin II. (of Courtenay) had ceded to his house, were so extensive and so menacing that Michael Palæologus thought there was only one course to pursue in order to avert the danger. He accepted the invitation addressed to him by Pope Gregory X., and sent representatives of the Greek Church to the Council of Lyons. There, on the 29th of June 1279, amidst much enthusiasm, the reconciliation of the Eastern and Western Churches was solemnly proclaimed.

This really did help to avert the danger and counteract the preparations of the ambitious King of Naples. The Greek diplomatists were highly pleased with the success of their move; the monks and the people of Constantinople only laughed at the performances of the Council; but in the end this insincere attempt at reconciliation produced greater estrangement, increasing among the Latins their disgust against what they called "the hypocrisy and duplicity of the Greeks."

But that which the embarrassed and short-sighted Byzantine leaders at the close of the thirteenth century

[1] Pachymeras has interesting details of these transactions.

considered only as a clever stroke of policy became an unavoidable necessity from the middle of the fourteenth century. |John Cantacuzene, who, with all his shortcomings and vanities, was an able statesman, recognised at once that the Turks were a far more formidable danger to the Greek Empire than either the Latins or the neighbouring Slavs.| He was the first to declare openly that an alliance with the warlike nations of the West could alone save the Greek Empire from the Turks. | From his time onwards the alliance with the Latins became the standing policy of the Byzantine statesmen. It was a policy imposed by force of circumstances. The orthodox kings of Bulgaria, Serbia, and Bosnia, were by the same circumstances led to seek for alliances with the Catholic kings of Hungary and Poland.

Some Greek, and especially some Russian historians cannot sufficiently blame Rome for its utilising the danger that threatened the Eastern Empire to impose the Papal authority on it. But it was only natural that the Popes should seize the opportunity to bring about the union of the Churches. It was impossible for them to act differently. It was for them a simple and unavoidable compliance with a sacred and self-evident duty. From their point of view, it was manifest that Providence had chosen to use the arms of the Infidels to break the stubbornness of the stiff-necked Greeks, and to compel them to bow before the successors of St Peter. In perfect good faith, the Popes thought it clearly their duty to co-operate with Providence for so good a purpose. Rome doing its duty added much to the melancholy character of this great tragedy.

6. But it was also quite natural that the masses of the orthodox people in Bosnia, Serbia, Bulgaria, and Greece, should not be able to comprehend the motives which produced the apparent inconsistency of their own rulers and statesmen. They had grown up and been systematically educated in the belief that the Roman Church was the enemy of their own national and truly orthodox Church, and that the Pope was an incarnate Anti-christ; they had been accustomed to give the name of "Rim-papa" to their dogs; they had been taught that the Latins were cheats, liars, and thieves, faithless and effeminate weaklings, who ate frogs, rats, and cats. And now, suddenly, their rulers came and declared to them that in consequence of a (probably exaggerated) danger from the Turks, they must unite their "Orthodox" Church with the "heretical" Church of Rome, acknowledge "Anti-christ" as "Christ's Vicar" on earth, and embrace as brothers the impure and barbarous Latins!

It was not an easy task for the Emperors of Byzantium and for their statesmen to suppress their own personal feelings, conquer their own prejudices, and accept with a good grace what seemed to be inevitable. Yet they did it. The Council of Florence in A.D. 1438 bears evidence of the readiness of some Greeks to sacrifice their dearest and deepest personal affections and convictions to the political interest of their country. But no earthly power was able to change the heart of the masses of the people, and to dispel the clouds of prejudices accumulated through so many generations. The populace execrated the union subscribed to by their Emperor and his great secular and ecclesiastic dignitaries. To the axiom of Gregory VII., "Better Islam than schism!" the Greeks of Constantinople now answered, "Better Islam than the Pope!" And Islam, turning towards Mecca, praised the only one and true God, who did not permit the Giaours to unite against the faithful !

17. To the wide-awake and wary Turkish Sultans it was quite clear that the real and practical alliance of the Balkanic with the Western nations would be the death-warrant of Turkish ambitions. Therefore to prevent such an alliance by every means became to the Porte a matter of immense importance.

Sometimes they succeeded in doing this by prompt military action. When it was reported to Murad I. that King Shishman of Bulgaria had entered into negotiations for an offensive and defensive alliance with King Lazar of Serbia and King Sigismund of Hungary, the Turks unexpectedly invaded Bulgaria, and destroyed her army, capturing Shishman and all the royal family in Nicopolis (A.D. 1386). There is no doubt that the great battle on the field of Kossovo (15th June 1389) was fought with the intention of paralysing Serbia before her ally, the King of Hungary, could come to her assistance. When, a few years later, Vuk Brankovich, prince of the country lying between Bosnia and Macedonia (now Kossovo-Eyalet), reopened negotiations with Hungary, the Turks prevented the accomplishment of his projects by suddenly seizing and poisoning him (1395). When, shortly afterwards, the young Prince of Serbia, Stephan, the son of Lazar, went personally to do homage to Bayazed Ilderim, the Sultan warned him against leaning toward Hungary, "*because,*" he said impressively, "*no good can come to those who lean that way; think what became of King Shishman and the other princes who sought alliances with Hungary!*" These words are quoted by Constantine, the Court chaplain of Prince Stephan Lazarevich, who had heard them probably from Stephan's, if not from the Sultan's own lips.[1]

That the Turks sought to prevent a Christian confederacy by diplomatic moderation and conciliation is shown by the counsels given to his sons by the Emperor John V. on his deathbed:—

"*Whenever the Turks begin to be troublesome, send embassies to the West at once, offer to accept union, and*

[1] Constantine the Philosopher, in his life of *Stephan the Tall*, in the *Glasnik*, vol. xxxiii. p. 172.

protract negotiations to great length; the Turks so greatly fear such union that they will become reasonable; and still the union will not be accomplished because of the vanity of the Latin nations!"

It will be seen that the much-abused Chalil-Pasha, Grand Vizier to Mohammed the Conqueror, acted in the spirit of the traditional diplomacy of his predecessors.

8. But from the death of John V. (1391) to the death of John VII. (1448) the Turks had become much stronger, better organized, and more fully informed. They had had opportunities of measuring themselves successfully against Hungarian, Polish, German, and French knights. They had been witnesses of the decay of the remaining strength of the old Empire; and they began to suspect that the threats of uniting the Western nations against them were vain vapourings. They were shrewd enough to perceive that the task of uniting all the Christian nations for a great and earnest effort was almost hopeless. While the Greeks were not learning anything, the Turks became stronger in offensive power and richer in practical knowledge of the true state of political circumstances in Europe.

And in truth, the very act by which the wisest amongst the Greek statesmen thought to guard their country against danger—the acceptance at the Council of Florence of the union of the Churches—

proved only a source of weakness. It brought no help from the West; yet it divided and paralysed what little strength remained at home. About the year 1450 Constantinople was in reality a "house divided against itself," which it is declared must fall.

The Christians of the East ought to have been assisted by the Christians of the West. But a strange fatality seems to have beset Christendom between the eleventh and fifteenth centuries. The Byzantine and the Latin worlds were in friction throughout those ages. The separation of Churches, the Crusades, the Latin conquest of Constantinople, the ambition of the Popes and of the Sicilian Kings, even the attempts at the reconciliation of Churches—all these contributed to disorganize the vital forces of the Byzantine Empire. Not merely did the Western Christians fail to come to the rescue of their Oriental brethren in the hour of need, but the Papal policy sapped the vigour of the ancient Empire of the East, and, unintentionally, yet not the less effectually, it laid the foundations of a secure establishment of a Mohammedan power in Europe.

CHAPTER II.

THE SUPERIOR MILITARY ORGANIZATION OF THE TURKS.

MORAL and political causes contributed to the remarkable quickness with which the Christian states of the Balkan Peninsula were subdued by the Turks.

But the instrument which chiefly wrought Turkish victories and Christian defeats was undoubtedly *the superior military organization of the Turks.*

Not one of the Christian kingdoms of the Balkan Peninsula had a regular standing army. The sovereigns of Bosnia, Serbia, Bulgaria, and Greece usually surrounded themselves with a more or less numerous body of guards, mostly professional soldiers hired abroad,—Germans, Italians, Normans, and sometimes (especially in thirteenth and fourteenth centuries) even Turks. The fidelity of these mercenaries could only be secured by the high rate of their pay, and this precluded the possibility of large numbers being permanently employed. An emperor's or a king's bodyguard rarely exceeded 3000 men. These household troops, being constantly under arms, were the nearest approach to a standing army amongst the Christian nations prior to the middle of the fifteenth century, when King Charles VII. of France enrolled his "Franc-Archers," the first regular army in a Christian country (A.D. 1449).

When a Christian king had to defend his own country, or to carry war into that of an enemy, he called his nobles to his aid, with as many men as they could collect and arm amongst their own tenants and retainers. This irregular soldiery might have had much personal courage, but they were generally badly armed, and certainly undisciplined. In fact, the more numerous they were, the more incongruous and incomplete was their equipment, and the less their willingness to submit to orders from head-quarters. The political disorders prevailing throughout the peninsula on the eve of the Turkish invasion had weakened this feudal military organization, which was already inherently weak. Tzar Lazar of Serbia felt it necessary to add to his war manifesto a long and terrible curse against all those who should not respond by joining him at the field of Kossovo.

The Turks had retained this feudal military system, defining more precisely the number of armed followers each feudal lord was bound to produce when called to the standard of the Sultan, (*Ziyamet* and *Timar Beys*).

Independently of this feudal army, the Turks possessed from 1326 *a regular standing army.* Orkhan and his brother Vezir Ala-ud-din inaugurated a system remarkable for its completeness and success, a system which testified to the great psychological insight and political foresight of its organizers. They not only converted military service into a permanent profession for life, but made it one for which men must be strictly trained from their boyhood. More than this, with an ingenuity which would be most admirable were it not almost satanic, these organizers did not dream of drawing the materials for their standing army from the ranks of the Turks. They decided that the force which was to conquer the Christian kingdoms and empires should be supplied by the foes of Islam!

From amongst the Christian children captured in war or in never-ceasing raids across the frontiers, the most healthy, handsome, and intelligent were selected and sent to special colleges. There they were trained to be zealous Mussulmen and intrepid soldiers, and when sufficiently prepared were enrolled in the regiments of the famous Janissaries.

Should the required number of physically and mentally qualified cadets not be recruited from among those captured and brought as slaves, special Imperial Commissioners levied the most cruel of tributes from the Christian Rayahs,—that of their most promising sons from seven to twelve years old. Thus the principle of selection was applied in a hitherto unheard-of manner, to refresh and strengthen the Turkish Empire by the best blood of the Christians.

The Janissaries (or more exactly " *Yeni-Cheri*," the

"new troops") were instituted as a standing regular army by Orkhan in 1326. They were reorganized by his son, Murad I., who, on that account, was believed by many early writers to be their original founder. How thoroughly and soundly based was this organization can be seen from the summary of rules prescribed by Murad, and thus set forth by Ahmed Djevad Bey[1]:—

1. The first duty of every Janissary is absolute obedience to the orders of his officers, even if these officers were freed slaves.

2. Amongst the men belonging to the "Odjak" (the Turkish name for the corps of Janissaries, meaning "chimney" or "hearth"), perfect union and concord must prevail, and therefore they should always dwell together.

3. As truly brave and gallant men, they must always abstain from every luxury, avoid every unbecoming deed, and be simple in everything.

4. They must never disregard the teachings of the Holy Hadji Bektash as to their prayers, and they must always scrupulously fulfil the duties of true Mussulmen.

5. The chiefs must exercise the greatest viligance that no one be admitted to the Odjak who has not been taken and brought up according to the law of "Devchirmé" (law on the tribute in children).

[1] *Etat militaire Ottoman depuis la fondation de l'Empire*, par Ahmed Djevad Bey. Paris, 1882, p. 66.

6. Advancement in the Odjak must always follow the order of seniority.

7. A Janissary should only be punished or even reprimanded by his superior officer.

8. Janissaries incapacitated by illness or age are to receive pensions from the Odjak.

9. Janissaries must not wear beards, and shall not be allowed to marry.

10. They ought never to be far distant from their ortas (barracks).

11. No Janissary should be allowed to learn a trade, or to work as an artisan. His exclusive occupation ought to be exercise in the art of war.

Many peculiar privileges were given them in order to enhance their *esprit de corps*. One of these was that, when on campaign, their tents should be placed immediately in front of the Sultan's tent, so that the Padishah necessarily passed through their tents in leaving, or returning to his own. Another privilege was that the capital punishment of a Janissary should never be executed in the day-time, or in public, but always at midnight, in the presence of a few officers, a cannon shot fired in the central barrack at the same time announcing to the Odjak that one who belonged to it had been removed from this world by the hands of Justice.

During the fourteenth and fifteenth centuries the corps of Janissaries never numbered more than 12,000 men.

But in physical condition, training, discipline and bravery, no troops in Europe could be compared with them. They were all foot soldiers, their principal arm being a bow. Some of them had in addition a scimitar, others a lance.

Besides this regular infantry, the Sultans had from an early date a body of regular cavalry called "Spahees," who were recruited in the same way as the Janissaries. In the fifteenth century they were armed with a scimitar, an iron mace (20 to 25 pounds in weight), and a bow.

The greatest attention was given to the sword exercise of both Janissaries and Spahees. Their scimitars were made of metal much superior to any then generally used in Europe, and by constant practice the Janissaries and Spahees learned to use these with marvellous dexterity. The Turkish saying that they won their Empire "by the sword" was literally true.

The Greeks were superior to the Turks only in naval manœuvres and in the use of "Greek fire"; the secret of this composition was jealously kept.

* * * * *

There are two Christian contemporaries who speak with authority on the Turkish army in the middle of the fifteenth century. One is the Italian Francesco Philelpho, the other is a Frenchman—Bertrandon de la Brocquière.

Philelpho, himself a knight and statesman, sojourned

some time at the Sultan's "Porte" as Greek Envoy. He certainly enjoyed good opportunities of knowing the true condition of the Turkish military forces, and he describes them in his memoranda to the King of France (dated 14th November 1461) and to the Doge of Venice (10th February 1464). According to him, the Sultan's army was composed of 12,000 Janissaries, 8000 Assabs (who were in his regular pay), 25,000 feudal troops levied in Europe and 15,000 levied in Asia,—altogether 60,000. The Janissaries were all archers; they also carried a small shield, and some of them had long lances. The feudal troops were all horsemen, armed with scimitars, maces, and small shields; some of their number had bows. "But," he adds, "this regular army of the Sultans was always preceded and followed in war by innumerable bands of irregular troops, composed mostly of shepherds from Thracia, Thessaly, and Mœsia, who, being under no restraint, proved the most cruel scourge in the Turkish invasions. Their arms were only crooked Turkish sabres. They carried with them plenty of ropes to bind the inhabitants of towns and villages, and then drove them to the slave-markets; the villages and towns they pillaged and burnt down before the regular army of the Sultan made its appearance."[1]

George Castriot Scanderbeg (+ 1468) indirectly confirms Philelpho's statement about the usual strength

[1] Francisci Philelphi, *Epistolæ*, vol. ii. p. 52.

of the Turkish army. According to his biographers,[1] he often stated "*that the whole army of the Albanian league hardly equals in numbers the fourth part of the Sultan's forces.*" As the Albanians were able in a few instances to muster 15,000 men, but generally had not more than 12,000, it may be concluded that Scanderbeg estimated the Turkish army at about 60,000 men.

But the true expert in military matters was Bertra dou de la Brocquière, Seigneur de Vieux Château, Councillor and First Equerry to the Duke of Burgundy, Philippe le Bon. He went in 1432 to visit the holy places of Palestine, and returned in 1433 overland, passing through Constantinople, Adrianople, Bulgaria, and Serbia. He wrote for his Duke a description of his journey, with a memorandum about ways and means for driving the Turks out of Europe.[2] His observations are generally shrewd and apparently true, and his judgment bears the stamp of impartiality. We will quote some of his statements concerning the Turks and their army.

"The conversation" (which he held at Belgrade with some German officers) "greatly astonished me, and caused me to make some reflections on the strange subjection in which the Turk keeps Macedonia,

---

[1] Demetrius Franco, *Vita Georgii Scanderbegi*, Venetia, 1480; Marinus Barletius, *De Vita ac Gestis Georgii Scanderbegi*, Roma, 1503.

[2] We use the English translation of the *Early Travels in Palestine*, edited by Thomas Wright, London, 1848, pp. 362-369.

Bulgaria, the Emperor of Constantinople, the Greeks, the Despot of Serbia, and his subjects. Such a dependence appeared to me a lamentable thing for Christendom; and as I lived with the Turks, and became acquainted with their manner of living and fighting, and have frequented the company of sensible persons who have observed them narrowly in their great enterprises, I am emboldened to write something concerning them, according to the best of my ability. . . . .

"I shall begin with what regards their persons, and say they are a tolerably handsome race, with long beards, but of moderate size and strength. I know well that it is a common expression to say 'as strong as a Turk'; nevertheless I have seen an infinity of Christians excel them when strength was necessary, and I myself, who am not of the strongest make, have, when circumstances required labour, found very many Turks weaker than I.

"They are diligent, willingly rise early, and live on little, being satisfied with bread badly baked, raw meat dried in the sun, milk curdled or not, honey, cheese, grapes, fruit, herbs, and even a handful of flour, with which they make a soup sufficient to feed six or eight for a day. Should they have a horse or a camel sick without hopes of recovery, they cut its throat and eat it. I have witnessed this many and many a time. They are indifferent as to where they sleep, and usually lie on the ground. Their dress consists of two or three cotton garments, thrown one over the other, which fall to their feet. Over these, again, they wear a mantle of felt, called a 'capinat.' This, though light, resists rain, and some capinats are very fine and handsome. Their boots come up to the knees, and they wear wide drawers, some of crimson velvet, others of silk or fustian and common stuffs. In war, or when travelling, to avoid being embarrassed by their gowns, they tuck the ends into their drawers, that they may move with greater freedom.

"Their horses are good, cost little in food, gallop well and for a long time. They keep them on short allowances, never feeding them but at night, and then giving them only five or six handfuls of barley with double the quantity of chopped straw, the whole put into a bag which hangs from the horse's ears. At break of day, they bridle, clean, and curry the horses, but never allow them to drink before mid-day. In the afternoon they drink whenever they find water, and also in the evening when they lodge or encamp: for they always halt early, and near a river if possible. During the night they are covered with felt or other stuffs. The horses are saddled and bridled à la *genette*. Their saddles are commonly very rich, but hollow, having pummels before and behind, with short stirrup-leathers and wide stirrups. . . . . The men sit deeply sunk in their saddles as in an arm-chair, their knees very high, a position in which they cannot resist a blow from a lance without being unhorsed. The arms of those who have any fortune are a bow, a small wooden shield, a sword, a heavy mace with a short handle and the thick end cut into many angles. This is a dangerous weapon when struck on the shoulders, or on an unguarded arm. Several use small wooden bucklers when they draw the bow.

"Their obedience to superiors is boundless. None dare disobey, even when their lives are at stake. And it is chiefly owing to this steady submission that such great exploits have been performed, and such vast conquest achieved.

"I have been assured that whenever the Christian powers have taken up arms against the tribes, the latter have always had timely information. In this case the Sultan has their march watched by men assigned for this purpose, and he lays wait for them with his army two or three days' march from the spot where he proposes to fight them. Should he think the opportunity favourable, he falls suddenly on them. For these occasions they have a particular kind of march, beaten on a large drum. When this signal is given, those who are to lead march quietly off, followed by the others with the same silence, without the file ever being interrupted, the horses and men having been so trained. Ten thousand Turks on such an occasion will make less noise than 100 men in the Christian armies. In their ordinary marches they always walk, but in these they always gallop; and as they are lightly armed, they will thus advance further from evening to daybreak than in three other days. They choose also no horses but such as walk fast and gallop for a long time, while we select only those that gallop well and with ease. It is by these forced marches that they have succeeded in surprising and completely defeating the Christians in their different wars.

"Their manner of fighting varies according to circumstances. When they find a favourable opportunity, they divide themselves into different detachments, and thus attack many parts of an army at the same time. This mode is particularly adapted when they are among woods or mountains, from the great facility they have for uniting together again. At other times they form ambuscades, and send out well-mounted scouts to observe the enemy. If their report be that he is not on his guard, they instantly form their plan and take advantage of the circumstance. Should they find the army well drawn up, they curvet round it within bow-shot, and, while thus prancing, shoot at the men and horses, and continue this manœuvre so long that they at last throw the enemy into disorder. If the opposing army attempt to pursue them, they fly, and disperse separately, even should only a fourth part of their own number be ordered against them; but it is in their flight that they are formidable, and it has been almost always then that they have defeated the Christians. In flying they have the adroitness to shoot their arrows so unerringly that they scarcely ever fail to hit man or horse. Each horseman has also on the pummel of his saddle a tabolcan. When the chief, or any one of his officers, perceives the pursuing enemy to be in disorder, he gives three strokes on this instrument; the others, on hearing it, do the same, and they are instantly formed round their chief, like so many hogs round the old one; and then, according to circumstances, they either receive the charge of the assailants, or fall on them by detachments and attack them simultaneously in different places. In pitched battles they employ a stratagem which consists of throwing fireworks among the cavalry to frighten the horses. They often place in their front a great body of dromedaries and camels, which are bold and vicious; these they drive before them on the enemy's line of horse and throw it into confusion. . . . .

"It is the policy of the Turks to have their armies twice as numerous as those of the Christians. This superiority of numbers augments their courage, and allows them to form different corps, and to make their attack on various parts at the same time. Should they once force an opening, they rush through in incredible crowds, and it is then a miracle if all be not lost. .... The Turkish lances are worth nothing; their archers are the best troops they have, and these do not shoot so strongly or so far as ours. They have a more numerous cavalry; and their horses, though inferior in strength to ours and incapable of carrying such heavy weights, gallop better, and skirmish for a longer time without losing their wind.

"I must own that in my various experiences I have always found the Turks frank and loyal, and when it was necessary to show courage, they have never failed. .... Their armies, I know, commonly consist of 200,000 men, but the greater part are on foot, and destitute of wooden shields, helmets, mallets, or swords; few, indeed, being completely equipped. They have, besides, amongst them a great number of Christians, who are forced to serve—Greeks, Bulgarians, Macedonians, Albanians, Slavonians, Wallachians, Servians, and other subjects of the despots of that country. All these people detest the Turk, because he holds them in a severe subjection; and should they see the Christians, and above all the French, march in force against the Sultan, I have not the slightest doubt but they would turn against him and do him great mischief."

* * * * *

There is an interesting version of the life of George Castriot Scanderbeg in an old Serbian manuscript not yet printed. It follows, on the whole, the lines of Marinus Barletius' work on Scanderbeg, but has some modifications and additions, which do not only enrich our stores of historical knowledge but impart to the whole local and national colour. In both works it is recorded that on a certain occasion Sultan Mohammed, desiring to dispel the anxiety of his Viziers and Pashas in consequence of rumours of a great European coalition against the Turks, made a speech comparing the Christians and the Turks. Very probably Mohammed never delivered the address attributed to him, but the comparison was certainly made as early as when Barletius' work was written (towards the end of the fifteenth century), and by a person who evidently knew well the circumstances of which he spoke.

"You have heard," the Sultan is made to say, "that the Christians have united against us. But fear not! Your heroism will be above theirs! You know well the unwashed Gyaours, and their ways and manners, which certainly are not fine. They are indolent, sleepy, easily shocked, inactive; they like to drink much and to eat much; in misfortunes they are impatient, and in times of good fortune proud and overbearing. They are lovers of repose, and do not like to sleep without soft feather-beds; when they have no women with them they are sad and gloomy;

and without plenty of good wine they are unable to keep counsel among themselves. They are ignorant of any military stratagems. They keep horses only to ride while hunting with their dogs; if one of them wishes to have a good war-horse, he sends to buy it from us. They are unable to bear hunger, or cold, or heat, effort and menial work. They let women follow them in the campaigns, and at their dinners give them the upper places, and they want always to have warm dishes. In short, there is no good in them.

"But you, my glorious fellows, you can show a great many good qualities. You do not think much of your life or your food. You sleep little, and for that you do not want beds; the earth is your dining-table and any board your bed; there is nothing you consider a hardship; there is nothing you think it impossible to do!

"And then, the Christians fight constantly among themselves, because every one desires to be a king, or a prince, or the first amongst them. One says to another: 'Brother, help thou me to-day against this Prince, and to-morrow I will help thee against that one!' Fear them not; there is no concord amongst them. Every one takes care of himself only; no one thinks of the common interest. They are quarrelsome, unruly, self-willed, and disobedient. Obedience to their superiors and discipline they have none, and yet everything depends on that!

"When they lose a battle they always say: 'We were not well prepared!' or 'This or that traitor has betrayed us!' or 'We were too few in number, and the Turks were far more numerous!' or 'The Turks came upon us without previous declaration of war, by misleading representations and treachery! They have occupied our country by turning our internal difficulties to their own advantage!'

"Well, that is what they say, being not willing to confess truly and rightly: '*God is on the side of the Turks! It is God who helps them, and therefore they conquer us!*'"[1]

[1] I have used the text of the Serbian MS., *Povyest o Gyurgyu Zrnoyevichu, narechenom Skenderbegu*, No. 418, 8vo, of the National Library in Belgrade.

CHAPTER III.

On the Eve of the Fall.

WHEN history raises the curtain to show us one of the most stirring tragedies in the life of nations—the conquest of a higher civilization by a lower one—our interest is naturally absorbed by the personalities who are working out the decrees of Fate. But the great historical tableaux—in which Constantine Palæologus so nobly personified an ancient and highly cultured Empire falling with dignity and honour, and a great conqueror, like Mohammed II., typified his wild and rough, yet energetic and deeply religious Asiatic race—can only gain in interest when we bear in mind that they are displayed amid surroundings of such extraordinary natural beauties as those of the Bosphorus.

We would like if we could present to our readers that wonderful picture of hill and valley, sunny glades and shadowed bays, of sea and sky, which has excited the admiration of all who have looked on it. Still more we should have liked to place before their eyes a true picture of Constantinople, and of the social and political life within its walls, on the eve of its heroic defence and final fall. But though the beauties of the Bosphorus are an inexhaustible source of inspiration for artists in modern times, the drawings and descriptions of the life and surroundings of Constantinople in the middle of the fifteenth century are extremely rare.

Still, we have a bird's-eye view of the city of Constantinople from the year 1422, and a plan of the city from the year 1493.

The bird's-eye view of Constantinople was made in the above-mentioned year by the Florentine engineer and artist, Christophore Buondelmonti. There are only three copies extant—one, in the Vatican, has as yet not been published; one in Venice, edited by Mr Sathas,[1] and the third in Paris, which was printed by Banduri[2] as early as 1711.

It appears, according to G. Critobulos, the Greek biographer of Mohammed II., that the Sultan, some time after the conquest of Constantinople, ordered the celebrated Greek geographer, Georgios Amyroutzes of Trebizonde, to prepare for him maps of the different countries of the world. It is believed that Amyroutzes made at the same time a great map of the city of Constantinople, and that it was this map which was shown to Dr Dickson in the library of the Seraglio. It is

---

[1] C. N. Sathas, *Monumenta Historiæ Hellenicæ*, Paris, 1888, vol. iii.

[2] Banduri, *Imperium Orientale*, Parisiis, 1711, vol. ii., p. 448. See also Dufresne, *Constantinopolis Christiana, seu Descriptio urbis Constantinopolitanæ qualis extitit sub imperatoribus Christianis*, Parisiis, 1780.

further believed that Gentile Bellini, who spent some time in the Seraglio painting a portrait of Sultan Suleyman, carried with him back to Venice a copy of the same plan. From this copy several other copies were made and published in numerous editions during the sixteenth century.[1]

It is very probable that between the city of Constantinople at the time of its conquest by the Turks in 1453 and the city such as it is depicted on the plan of 1422 there could be hardly any material difference. The resources of the Byzantine Emperors between 1420 and 1453 were used principally in repairing and strengthening the city walls. On some stones, which have been taken when the Charsias Gate was pulled down, and which are now preserved in the Arsenal of Constantinople, there are inscriptions which state that the Emperor John Palæologus renovated the whole fortification of the town. This work was undertaken after the last siege by Murad II. in 1432. On one of the stones there is beneath the name of the Emperor the name of Manuel Jagaris (a Palæologue himself), which is believed to be that of the chief engineer who had charge of the restoration.[2] George Brankovich, the Prince of Serbia, the friend and ally of the Greek Emperors, reconstructed in the year 1448 at his own

---

[1] See also *Ancien plan de Constantinople, imprimé entre* 1566 *et* 1574, *avec notes explicatives par Cœdicius*, Constantinople, Lorentz et Keil, 1882.

[2] Dethier, *Der Bosphor und Constantinopel*, Wien, 1873, p. 55.

expense two towers in the walls of Constantinople; one in the wall along the Marmara Sea at the gate called at present Koum-Capou, and the other in the wall along the Golden Horn.[1] All these works, however, did not involve any material change in the principal lines and general character of the fortifications and the town itself such as it was when Buondelmonti sketched his plan, and such as it most probably was when the siege of 1453 took place.

It would be not less desirable to obtain an insight into the inner life of the old Greek capital on the eve of its fall. Fortunately we can satisfy this desire, at least in a certain measure. Chevalier Bertrandon de la Brocquière spent some time in Constantinople in 1433, and wrote for his master an interesting report of what he saw there.

Brocquière was one of the sharpest and most intelligent observers who travelled over that route in the Middle Ages; and as he was a soldier by profession, and a gentleman by birth and education, his observations are invaluable for the history of the Balkan Peninsula in the first half of the fifteenth century. He had the pluck and enterprising energy of a modern American

---

[1] The full inscription in Greek that the "Pyrgos" and the adjoining "cortina" at Koum-Capou were restored at the expense of George Brankovich, is given in Dr Mordtman, *Belagerung*, p. 132, and in Miklosich, *Monumenta Serbica*, p. 441. About the tower on the Golden Horn, see Novakovich, *Glas*, Journal of the Serb. Academy, vol. xix. p. 9.

reporter, and a decided talent to give most graphic description of all he saw. This is his picture of Constantinople as he saw it, January 1433:—

"We arrived at Scutari on the Straits and opposite to Pera. The Turks guard this passage, and receive a toll from all who cross it. My companions and I crossed in two Greek vessels. The owners of my boat took me for a Turk and paid me great honours; but when they saw me after landing leave my horse at the gate of Pera to be taken care of, and inquire after a Genoese merchant named Christopher Parvesin, to whom I had letters, they suspected I was a Christian. Two of them waited for me at the gate, and when I returned for my horse they demanded more than I had agreed on for my passage. I believe they would have even struck me if they had dared to do so: but I had my sword and my good tarquais, and a Genoese shoemaker, who lived hard by, coming to my assistance, they were forced to retreat. I mention this as a warning to travellers who, like myself, may have anything to do with the Greeks. All those with whom I have had any business have only made me more suspicious, and I have found more probity in the Turks. These Greeks do not love the Christians of the Roman Church, and the submission which they have since made to this Church was more through self-interest than sincerity.[1]

[1] Evidently Brocquière wrote his *Memoirs* after the nominal

"Pera is a large town, inhabited by Greeks, Jews, and Genoese. The last are masters of it under the Duke of Milan, who styles himself 'Lord of Pera.' It has a Podesta and other officers, who govern it after their manner. Great commerce is carried on with the Turks. The latter have a singular privilege, namely, that should any of their slaves run away and seek an asylum in Pera, they must be given back. The port is the handsomest I have seen, and I believe I may add of any in the possession of the Christians, for the largest Genoese vessels can lie alongside the quays. However, it seems to me that on the land side and near the church, in the vicinity of the gate at the extremity of the haven, the place is weak.

"I met at Pera an ambassador from the Duke of Milan, named Sir Benedicto de Furlino. The Duke, wanting the support of the Emperor Sigismund against the Venetians, and seeing Sigismund embarrassed with the defence of his kingdom of Hungary against the Turks, had sent an embassy to Amurath, to negotiate a peace between the two princes. Sir Benedicto, in honour of my Lord of Burgundy, gave me a gracious reception. He even told me that, to do mischief to the Venetians, he had contributed to make them lose Salonica, taken from them by the Turks; and certainly in this he acted so much the worse, for I have since

reconciliation of the Greek and Roman Churches at the Council of Florence in 1438.

D

seen the inhabitants of that town deny Jesus Christ and embrace the Mohammedan religion.

"Two days after my arrival at Pera I crossed the haven to Constantinople, to visit that city. It is large and spacious, having the form of a triangle; one side is bounded by the straits of St George, another towards the south by the bay, which extends as far as Gallipoli, and at the north side is the port. There are, it is said, three large cities on the earth, each enclosing seven hills—Rome, Constantinople, and Antioch. Rome is, I think, larger and more compact than Constantinople.

"They estimate the circuit of the city of Constantinople at eighteen miles, a third of which is on the land side towards the west. It is well enclosed with walls, particularly on the land side. This extent, estimated at six miles from one angle to the other, has likewise a deep ditch, excepting for about two hundred paces at one of its extremities near the palace called Blaquerne. I was assured that the Turks had failed in their attempt to take the town at this weak point. Fifteen or twenty feet in front of this ditch there is a good and high wall. At the two extremities of this line were formerly handsome palaces, which, if we may judge from their present ruins, were also very strong. . . . .

"Constantinople is formed of many separate parts, so that it contains several open spaces of greater extent than those built on. The largest vessels can anchor under its walls, as at Pera. It has, beside, a small harbour in the interior, capable of containing three or four galleys. This is situated to the southward near a gate, where a hillock is pointed out composed of bones of the Christians, who, after the conquests of Jerusalem and Acre by Godfrey de Bouillon, were returning by this strait. When the Greeks had ferried them over, they conducted them to this place, which is remote and secret, and there the Crusaders were murdered. . . . But as this is an old story, I know of it no more than what was told me.

"The city has many handsome churches, but the most remarkable and the principal church is that of St Sophia, where the Patriarch resides, with others of the rank of Canons. It is of a circular shape, situated near the eastern point, and formed of three different parts: one subterranean, another above the ground, and a third over that. Formerly it was surrounded by cloisters, and had, it is said, three miles in circumference. It is now of smaller extent, and only three cloisters remain, all paved and inlaid with squares of white marble, and ornamented with large columns of various colours. The gates are remarkable for their breadth and height, and are of brass. This church, I was told, possesses one of the robes of our Lord, the end of the lance that pierced His side, the sponge that was offered Him to drink from, and the reed that was put into His hand. I can only say that behind the choir I was shown the gridiron on which St Laurence was broiled, and a large stone in the shape of a wash-stand, on which they say Abraham gave the angels food when they were going to destroy Sodom and Gomorrah.

"I was curious to witness the manner of the Greeks when performing divine service, and went to St Sophia on a day when the Patriarch officiated. The Emperor was present, accompanied by his consort, his mother, and his brother the Despot of Morea.[1] A mystery was represented, the subject of which was the three youths whom Nebuchadnezzar had ordered to be thrown into the fiery furnace. The Empress, daughter to the Emperor of Trebizonde, seemed very handsome; but as I was at a distance, I wished to have a nearer view. And I was also desirous to see how she mounted her horse, for it was thus she had come to the church, attended only by two ladies, three elderly men, ministers of state, and three of that species of men to whose guard the Turks entrust their wives. On coming out of St Sophia, the Empress went into an adjoining house to dine, which obliged me to wait until she returned to her palace, and consequently to pass the whole day without eating or drinking.

[1] The Emperor was John Palæologus, the Despot of Morea his brother Demetrius, his mother the Empress Irene, the daughter of the Serbian Prince Constantine Dragash, and the Emperor's consort was Maria Comnena, daughter of Alexis Comnena, Emperor of Trebizonde. She died on the 17th December 1439.

"At length she appeared. A bench was brought forth and placed near her horse, which was superb, and had a magnificent saddle. When she had mounted the bench, one of the old men took the long mantle she wore, passed to the opposite side of the horse, and held it in his hand extended as high as he could; during this she put her foot in the stirrup, and bestrode the horse like a man. When she was in her seat, the old man cast the mantle over her shoulders; after which one of those long hats with a point, so common in Greece, was given to her; at one of the ends it was ornamented with three golden plumes, and was very becoming. I was so near that I was ordered to fall back, and consequently had a full view of her. She wore in her ears broad and flat earrings, set with precious stones, especially rubies. She looked young and fair and handsomer than when in church. In one word, I should not have had a fault to find with her, had she not been painted, and assuredly she had no need of it. The two ladies also mounted their horses; they were both handsome, and wore mantles and hats like the Empress. The company returned to the palace of Blaquerne.

"In the front of St Sophia is a large and fine square, surrounded with walls like a palace, where in ancient times games were performed. I saw the brother of the Emperor, the Despot of Morea, exercising himself there with a score of other horsemen. Each had a bow, and they galloped along the inclosure, throwing their hats before them, which, when they had passed, they shot at; and he who pierced his hat with an arrow, or was nearest to it, was esteemed the most expert. This exercise they have adopted from the Turks, and it was one in which they were endeavouring to make themselves efficient.

"On this side, near the point of the angle, is the beautiful church of St George, which has, facing Turkey in Asia, a tower at the narrowest part of the straits. On the other side, to the westward, is a very high square column with characters traced on it, and an equestrian statue of Constantine in bronze on the summit. He holds a sceptre in his left hand, and holds his right extended towards Turkey in Asia and the road to Jerusalem, as if to denote that the whole of that country was under his rule. Near this column there are three others placed in a line, and each of one block. Here stood once three gilt horses, now at Venice.

"In the pretty church of Pantheocrator, occupied by Greek monks, who are what we should call in France Gray Franciscan Friars, I was shown a stone or table of divers colours, which Nicodemus had caused to be cut for his own tomb, and on which he laid out the body of our Lord, when he took Him down from the cross. During this operation the Virgin was weeping over the body, but her tears, instead of remaining on it, fell on the stone, and they are all now to be seen upon it. At first I took them for drops of wax, and touched them with my hand, and then bent down to look at them horizontally and against the light, when they seemed to me like drops of congealed water. This is a thing that may have been seen by many persons as well as by myself. In the same church are the tombs of Constantine and of St Helena his mother, each raised about 8 feet high on a column, having their summit terminated in a point, cut into four sides, in the fashion of a diamond. It is said that the Venetians, while in power at Constantinople, took the body of St Helena from its tomb and carried it to Venice, where, they say, it is still preserved. It is further said that they attempted the same thing in regard to the body of Constantine, but could not succeed; and this is probable enough, for to this day two broken parts of the tomb are to be seen, where they made the attempt. The tombs are of red jasper.

" In the church of St Apostles is shown the broken shaft of the column to which our Saviour was fastened when He was beaten with rods by order of Pilate. This shaft, above the height of a man, is of the same stone as the two others that I have seen at Rome and at Jerusalem; but this one exceeds in height the others put together. There are likewise in the same church many holy relics in wooden coffins, and any one who chooses may see them. One of the saints had his head cut off, and to his skeleton the head of another saint has been placed. The Greeks, however, have not the like devotion that we have for such relics. It is the same with respect to the stone of Nicodemus and the pillar of our Lord, which last is simply enclosed by planks, and placed upright near one of the columns on the right hand of the great entrance at the front of the church.

"Among several beautiful churches I will mention only yet one as remarkable, namely, that which is called Blaquerna from being near the imperial palace, which, although small and badly roofed, has paintings, and a pavement inlaid with marble. I doubt not that there may be others worthy of notice, but I was unable to visit them all. The Latin merchants have one situated opposite to the passage to Pera, where mass is daily read after the Roman manner.

"There are merchants from all nations in this city, but none so powerful as the Venetians, who have a bailiff to regulate all their affairs independently of the Emperor and his ministers. This privilege they have enjoyed for a long time. It is even said that they have twice by their galleys saved the town from the Turks; but for my part I believe that they spared it more for the holy relics' sake it contains than anything else. The Turks also have an officer to superintend their commerce, who, like the Venetian bailiff, is independent of the Emperor. They have even the privilege, that if one of their slaves should run away and take refuge within the city, on their demanding him, the Emperor is bound to give him up. This prince must be under great subjection to the Turk, since he pays him, I am told, a tribute of ten thousand ducats annually. And this sum is only for Constantinople, for beyond that town he possesses nothing but a castle situated three leagues to the north, and in Greece a small city called Salubria.

"I was lodged with a Catalonian merchant, who having told one of the officers of the palace that I was attached to my Lord of Burgundy, the Emperor caused me to be asked if it were true that the Duke had taken the Maid of Orleans, which the Greeks would scarcely believe. I told them truly what had happened, at which they were greatly astonished.

"The merchants informed me that on Candlemas-day there will be a solemn service performed in the afternoon, similar to what we perform on that day, and they conducted me to the church. The Emperor was at one end of the hall, seated on a cushion. The Empress viewed the ceremony from an upper window. The chaplains who chant the service are strangely and richly dressed; they sing the service by heart.

"Some days after they took me to see a feast given on the marriage of one of the Emperor's relatives. There was a tournament after the manner of the country, which appeared very strange to me. I will describe it. In the middle of a square they had planted a large pole, to which was fastened a plank 3 feet wide and 5 feet high. Forty cavaliers advanced to the spot, without any arms or armour whatever but a short stick. They at first amused themselves by running after each other, which lasted for about half an hour. Then from sixty to eighty rods of elder were brought, of the thickness and length of those we use for thatching. The bridegroom first took one and set off full gallop towards the plank to break it; as the rod shook in his hand, he broke it with ease, when shouts of joy resounded, and the instruments of music, namely nacaires, like those of the Turks, began to play. Each of the other cavaliers broke their wands in the same manner. Then the bridegroom tied two of them without being wounded! Thus ended the feast, and everyone returned home safe and sound. The Emperor and Empress have been spectators of this entertainment from a window.

"My intention was to leave Constantinople with this Sir Benedict de Furlino, who, as I have said, was sent as ambassador to the Turks by the Duke of Milan. There was a gentleman named Jean Visconti and seven other persons in his suite. He had ten horses loaded with baggage, for a traveller through Greece must absolutely carry everything requisite with him. We departed from Constantinople on the 23rd January 1433."

To this sketch of the Greek capital we may give as a "pendant" Brocquière's impressions of the Sultan's Court at Adrianople, and of the Turks in general. The French knight had twice to cross the whole breadth of Macedonia, as Sultan Murad II. happened to be at that time at Larissa in Thessaly. The picture which Brocquière's *Journal* unrolls before our eyes is one of great desolation. On the whole stretch, from Burgas on the Black Sea to Yenige-Basar, the country was covered with ruins of towns and castles, and most villages were empty and abandoned. It was, so to say, on the second day after the great wave of Turkish invasion had passed across that once so happy and well-populated country, that our French knight travelled through Thracia and Macedonia. But let him resume his own report.

"We did not proceed to Larissa, for, having heard that the Grand Turk was on his way back, we waited for him at Yenige-Basar, a village constructed by his subjects. When he (the Sultan) travels, his escort consists of four or five hundred horse; but as he is passionately fond of hawking, the greater part of his troop was composed of falconers and goshawk-trainers, who are great favourites with him, and I was told he keeps more than two thousand of them. Having this passion, he travels very short days' journeys, which are to him more an object of amusement and pleasure. He entered Yenige-Basar in a shower of rain, having only fifty horsemen attending him, and a dozen archers, his slaves, walking on foot before him. His dress was a robe of crimson velvet, lined with sable, and on his head he wore, like the Turks, a red hat. To save himself from the rain he had thrown over his robe another in the manner of a mantle after the fashion of the country.

"He was encamped in a tent which had been brought with him, for lodgings are nowhere to be found, nor any provision, except in the large towns, so that travellers are obliged to carry all things with them. The Sultan had numbers of camels and other beasts of burden. In the afternoon he left his tent to go to bathe, and I saw him at my ease. He was on horseback, with the same hat and crimson robe, attended by six persons on foot. I heard him speak to his attendants, and he seemed to have a deep-toned voice. He is about twenty-eight or thirty years old, and is already very stout.

"The ambassador sent one of his attendants to ask him if he could have an audience, and present him with gifts he had brought. He gave answer that being now occupied with his pleasures, he is not prepared to listen to any matters of business; that, besides, his bashaws were absent, that the ambassador must wait for them or return to Adrianople. Sir Benedict accepted the latter proposal, and consequently we returned to Carmissin, whence, having again crossed a great mountain, we entered a road made between two high rocks, through which a river flows. A strong castle, called Coloung, had been built on one of these rocks, but is now in ruins. The mountain is partly covered with wood, and is inhabited by a wicked race of cut-throats.

"At length we arrived at Trajanopoly, a town built by the Emperor Trajan, who did many things worthy of record. This town was very large, near the sea and the Maritza; but now has only a few inhabitants, being almost entirely in ruins. A mountain rises to the east of it, and the sea lies on the south. One of its baths bears the name of Holy Water. Further on is Vyra, an ancient castle, demolished in many places. A Greek told me the church had three hundred canons attached to it. The choir still remains, but the Turks have converted it into a mosque. They have also surrounded the castle with a considerable town, inhabited by them and the Greeks. It is situated on a mountain near the Maritza.

"On leaving Vyra, we met the Lieutenant of Greece (the Beyler Bey of Roumelia), whom the Sultan had sent for, and who was now hurrying with a troop of one hundred and twenty horsemen to join his master. He is a handsome man, a native of Bulgaria, had been the slave of his master, but as he had proved to be able to drink hard, the Sultan raised him to be the Governor of Greece, with a revenue of fifty thousand ducats.

"We had to wait eleven days in Adrianople. At length the Sultan arrived on the first day of Lent. The Mufti, who is to them what the Pope is to us, went out to meet him, accompanied by the principal persons of the town, who formed a long procession. The Sultan was already near the town when they met him, but had halted to take some refreshment, and had sent forward some of his attendants. He did not make his entry until nightfall.

"During my stay in Adrianople I had the opportunity of making acquaintance with several persons who had resided at the Turkish Court, and consequently knew the Sultan well, and who told me many particulars about him. In the first place, as I have seen him frequently, I shall say that he is a little, short, thick-set man, with the face of a Tartar. He has a broad and brown face, high cheek-bones, a round beard, a big and crooked nose, and small eyes. But I was told that he was kind, good, generous, and willingly gives away lands and money. His revenues are two millions and a half of ducats, including two hundred and fifty thousand received as tribute money. Besides, when he raises an army, it not only costs him nothing, but he gains by it; for the troops that are brought him from Asia pay for the transport to Gallipoli three aspers for each man, and five for each horse. It is the same at the passage of the Danube. Whenever his soldiers go on an expedition, and make a capture of slaves, he has the right of choosing one out of every five. He is, nevertheless, thought not to love war, and this report seems to me well founded. He has, in fact, hitherto met with such trifling resistance from Christendom, that, were he to employ all his power and wealth on this object, it would be easy for him to conquer great part of it. His favourite pleasures are hunting and hawking, and he has, I was told, upwards of a thousand hounds, and two thousand trained hawks of different sorts, of which I have seen very many. He loves liquor, and those who drink hard. As for himself, he can easily quaff off from ten to twelve gondils of wine, which means six or seven quarts. When he has drunk much, he becomes generous, and distributes his great gifts; his attendants therefore are very happy when they hear him call for wine. Last year a Maure took it into his head to preach to him on this subject, reminding him that wine was forbidden by the Prophet, and that those who drink it are not good Mussulmen. The only answer the Sultan gave was to order him to prison; he then expelled him from his territories, with orders never again to set his foot on them. He has great love for women, of whom he has three hundred. He gave his own sister for wife to one of his pages, with an annual income of 25,000 ducats. Some persons estimate his treasure at half a million of ducats, others at a million. This is exclusive of his plate, his slaves, his jewels for his women, which last article is estimated alone at a million of gold. I am convinced that if he would for one year abstain from thus giving away blindly, and hold his hand, he would lay by a million of ducats without wronging any one.

"Every now and then he makes great and remarkable examples of justice, which procure him perfect obedience at home and abroad. He likewise knows how to keep his country in an excellent state of defence, without oppressing his Turkish subjects by taxes or other modes of extortion. His household is composed of five thousand persons, as well horsemen as footmen. But in the war-time he does not augment their pay, so that he does not expend more than in time of peace, contrary to what happens in other countries. His principal officers are three Bashaws or Vizier-Bashaws. The Vizier is a counsellor, the Bashaw a sort of chief. These three have the charge of all that concern him or his household, and no one can speak with him but through them. When he is in Greece (viz., in the Balkan Peninsula) the Lieutenant of Greece has superintendence of the army; and when in Turkey (viz., Asia Minor), the Lieutenant of Turkey (Anadoly Beyler Bey). He has given away great possessions, but he may resume them at pleasure. Besides, those to whom they have been given are bound to serve him in war with a certain number of troops at their own expense. It is thus that Greece annually supplies him with thirty thousand men, whom he may lead whither he pleases; and Turkey ten thousand, for whom he only has to find provisions. Should he want a more considerable army, Greece alone, as I was assured, can supply him with one hundred and twenty thousand more; but he is obliged to pay for these. The pay is five aspers for the infantry, and eight for the cavalry. I have, however, heard that of these hundred and twenty thousand, there was but half—that is to say, the cavalry—that were properly equipped and well armed with shields and swords; the rest were composed of men on foot, miserably accoutred, some having swords without bows, others without swords, bows, or any arms whatever, many having only staves. It is the same with the infantry supplied by Turkey, one half of them being armed with staves. This Turkish infantry is nevertheless more esteemed than the Greek, and the men are generally considered as better soldiers.

"Other persons whose testimony I regard as authentic have since told me, that the troops Turkey is obliged to furnish, when the Sultan wants to form an army, amount to thirty thousand men and those from Greece to twenty thousand, without including two or three thousand slaves of his own, whom he arms well. Amongst these slaves are many Christians, and there are likewise numbers of them amongst the troops from Greece—Albanians, Bulgarians, and men from other

E

countries too. In the last army from Greece, there were three thousand Servian horsemen, which the Despot of Servia had sent under the command of one of his sons. It was with great regret that these people came to serve him, but they dared not refuse.

"The Bashaws arrived at Adrianople three days after their lord, bringing with them part of his people and his baggage. For the transport of this baggage they used about a hundred camels, and two hundred and fifty mules and horses, as amongst these people waggons are not used.

"Sir Benedict was impatient to have an audience, and made inquiries of the Bashaws if he could see the Sultan. Their answer was in the negative. The reason of this refusal was that they had been drinking with him and were all intoxicated. They, however, sent on the morrow to the ambassador, to let him know they were visible, when he instantly waited on each with his presents; for such is the custom of the country that no one can speak to them without bringing a gift; even the slaves who guard their gates are not exempted from it. I accompanied him on this visit. On the following day he was informed that he might come to the palace. He instantly mounted his horse to go thither with his attendants, and I joined the company. But we all were on foot, he alone being on horseback.

"In front of the court we found a great number of

men and horses. The gate was guarded by about thirty slaves, under the command of a chief, armed with staves. Should any person try to enter without permission, they bid him retire; if he persists, they drive him away with their staves. What we call 'The Court of the King' the Turks call 'The Gate of the Lord.' Every time the Sultan receives a message or an embassy, which happens almost daily, he 'keeps the gate.'

"When the ambassador had entered, they made him sit down near the gate with many other persons who were waiting for the Sultan to quit his apartment and hold his court. The three Bashaws first entered, with the Governor of Greece and others of the great lords. The Sultan's rooms looked into a very large court, and the Governor went thither to wait for him. At length he (the Sultan) appeared. His dress was, as usual, a crimson satin robe, over which he had, by way of mantle, another of green figured satin, lined with sable. His young boys accompanied him, but no further than to the entrance of the apartment, and then returned. There was nobody with him but a small dwarf and two young persons who acted the part of fools. He walked across the angle of the court to a gallery, where a seat had been prepared for him. It was a kind of raised couch, covered with velvet, with four or five steps leading up to it. He seated himself on it as do our tailors when they are going to work, and the three Bashaws placed themselves a little way from him. The other officers, who on these days form part of his attendants, likewise entered the gallery and posted themselves along the walls, as far from him as they could. Without, but facing him, were twenty Wallachian gentlemen seated, who had been detained as hostages for the good conduct of their countrymen. Within this apartment were placed about a hundred dishes of tin, each containing some mutton and rice. When all were placed, a lord from Bosnia was introduced, who pretended that the crown of that country belonged to him, and came in consequence to do homage for it to the Sultan, and ask succour from him against its present king. He was conducted to a place near the Bashaws, and when his attendants had made their appearance, the ambassador from Milan was sent for. He advanced, followed by the men bearing his presents, which were set down near the tin dishes. Persons appointed to receive them held them above their heads as high as they could, that the Sultan and his Court might see them. While this was passing Sir Benedict walked slowly toward the gallery. A person of distinction came forward to introduce him. On entering, Sir Benedict made an obeisance, without taking off the hat from his head, and when near the steps of the couch he made another very low bow. The Sultan then rose, descended two steps to come nearer to the ambassador, and took him by the hand.

The envoy wished to kiss his hand, but he declined the homage, and through a Jew interpreter, who spoke the Jewish and Italian languages, asked how his good brother and neighbour, the Duke of Milan, fared in health. The ambassador having replied to this question, was conducted to a seat near the Bosnian, walking backwards with his face towards the Sultan, according to the custom of the country. The Sultan waited to see the ambassador sit down, and then re-seated himself. Then the different officers who were on duty in the hall sat down on the floor, and the person who had introduced the ambassador came to fetch us, his attendants, and placed us near the Bosnians. In the meantime a silken napkin was attached to the Sultan, and a round piece of thin red leather was placed before him, for their usage is to eat only from table-coverings of leather. Then some dressed meat was brought to him in two gilt dishes. When he was served, his officers went and took the tin dishes spoken of, and distributed them to the persons in the hall, one dish among four. There was in each some mutton and rice, but neither bread nor anything to drink. I saw, however, in a corner of the court, a high buffet with shelves, which had some plates on them, and there was also a large silver vase, in the shape of a drinking-cup, out of which I saw many drink, but whether water or wine I know not. With regard to the meat on the dishes, some tasted it, others did not; but before all were served, it was necessary to take it away, for the Sultan was not inclined to eat. He never took anything in public, and there are very few persons who can boast of having heard him speak, or having seen him eat or drink. On his going away, the musicians who were standing in the court near the buffet began to play. They played on instruments, and sang songs about the heroic actions of Turkish warriors. When those in the gallery heard anything that pleased them, they shouted, after their manner, most horrid cries. Being ignorant on what they were playing, I went into the court, and saw it was on stringed instruments of a large size. The musicians entered the hall and ate whatever they could find. At length the meat was taken away, when every one rose up, and the ambassador retired, without having said a word respecting his embassy, which is never customary at a first audience. There is also another custom, that when an ambassador has been presented to the Sultan, the latter, until he shall have given him his answer, sends him wherewith to pay his daily expenses, the sum being two hundred aspers per day. On the next day, therefore, one of the officers of the Treasury, the same who conducted Sir Benedict to the Court, arrived with the above sum. Shortly after, the slaves who guarded the gate presented themselves for what is usually given to them. They are, however, satisfied with a trifle.

"On the third day the Bashaws let the ambassador know that they were ready to hear from him the subject of his embassy. He immediately went to the Court, and I accompanied him. But the Sultan had closed his audience, and was just retiring, and only the three Bashaws, with the Beyler Bey or Governor of Greece, now remained. When we had passed the gate, we found these four seated on a piece of wood that happened to be outside of the gallery. They sent to desire the ambassador would come forward, and had a carpet placed on the ground before them, on which they made him seat himself, like a criminal before his judges, notwithstanding there were great numbers of people present. He explained to them the object of his mission, which was, as I heard, to entreat their lord, on the part of the Duke of Milan, to consent to yield up to the Roman Emperor Sigismund, Hungary, Wallachia, Bulgaria as far as Sofia, Bosnia, and the part of Albania he now held, and which was dependent on Sclavonia. They replied they could not at that moment inform the Sultan of this request, as he was occupied, but that within ten days the ambassador would be informed of the Sultan's answer. There is likewise another custom, that from the time when an ambassador is announced as such, he can never speak with the Sultan personally. This regulation was made since the grandfather of the present Sultan was murdered by an ambassador from Serbia. That envoy had come to solicit from him some alleviation in favour of his countrymen, whom the Sultan wanted to reduce to slavery. In despair at not obtaining his object, he stabbed him, and was himself massacred the instant after.

"On the tenth day we went to the Court to receive the answer. The Sultan was there, again seated on his couch; but he had with him in the gallery only those that served his table. I saw neither buffet, minstrels, nor the Lord of Bosnia, nor the Wallachians, but only Magnoly, brother to the Duke of Cephalonia, whose manners towards the Sultan were those of a respectful servant. Even the Bashaws were without and standing at a distance, as well as the greater part of persons whom I had before seen in the hall, only that their number was now much smaller. While we were waiting outside, the Chief Cadi, with his assessors, administered justice at the outward gate of the palace, and I saw some foreign Christians come to plead their cause before him. But when the Sultan rose up, the judges ended their sittings, and retired to their homes. I saw the Sultan pass with his attendants to the great court, which I was unable to see on the first occasion. He wore a robe of cloth of gold and green, somewhat rich, and he seemed to me to have a hasty step. When he had re-entered his apartment, the Bashaws, having taken seat on that piece of wood as on the preceding day, sent for the ambassador. Their answer was that their master charged him to salute in his name his brother, the Duke of Milan, that he was very anxious of doing much for him, but that his present request was unreasonable; that from regard for him their master had frequently abstained from pushing his conquests further into Hungary, which he might easily have done, and such a sacrifice ought to satisfy him (the Duke of Milan); that it would be too much to expect the Sultan to surrender all he had won by sword; that under the present circumstances he and his soldiers had no other theatre where to display than the territories of the Emperor, and that he should be the more unwilling to renounce it as hitherto he had never met the Emperor's forces without vanquishing them or putting them to flight, as was well known to all the world.

"The ambassador, in fact, knew personally that all this was true, for in the last defeat of Sigismund before Golubatz he had witnessed his discomfiture; he had even the night preceding the battle quitted the Emperor's camp to wait on the Sultan.

"The ambassador having received this answer from the Bashaws, returned to his lodgings. But he was scarcely arrived when he received five thousand aspers, which the Sultan sent him, together with a robe of crimson camocas, lined with yellow calimanco. Thirty-six aspers are worth a Venetian ducat. But of those five thousand aspers the Sultan's treasurer retained ten per cent. as fees of his office.

During my stay at Adrianople I saw also a present of another sort made likewise by the Sultan, to a bride on her wedding-day. This bride was the daughter of the Beyler Bey, Governor of Greece. A daughter of one of the Bashaws was entrusted with carrying the Sultan's present to the bride. She was attended by upwards of thirty other women. Her own dress was of crimson tissue and gold; her face was covered, according to custom, with a very rich veil ornamented with diamonds. The attendant ladies had magnificent veils, and their dresses were robes of crimson velvet and of cloth of gold without fur. They were all on horseback, riding astride like men, and some of them had superb saddles. In front of the procession rode thirteen or fourteen horsemen and two minstrels, also on horseback, as well as other musicians, carrying a trumpet, a very large drum, and about eight pairs of cymbals, which altogether made a most abominable noise. After the musicians came the carriers of the presents, and then the ladies. The presents consisted of seventy broad platters of tin, laden with different sorts of sweetmeats, and of twenty other platters, having on them sheep, skinned, painted red and white and ornamented with silver rings suspended from the nose and ears.

"While at Adrianople I had an opportunity of seeing

numbers of Christians chained who were brought thither for sale. They begged for alms in the streets; but my heart bleeds when I think of the shocking hardships they suffer."

Brocquière left Adrianople in the suite of Sir Benedict on the 12th March. We will not follow him on his journey through Macedonia, Bulgaria, and Serbia, though his description of the same is full of interest, giving, as it does, graphic sketches of the country and the people, as well as of the incidents, which throw sufficient light on the true condition of the Balkan Peninsula shortly before the fall of Constantinople.[1]

[1] See *Voyage d'Outre-mer et Retour de Jerusalem on France par la voie de terre pendent le cours des années 1432 et 1433*, par Bertrandon de la Brocquière, conseiller et premier écuyer tranchant de Philippe le Bon, Duc de Bourgogne ; *Ouvrage extrait d'un manuscript de la bibliothèque nationale, remis en français moderne et publié*, par le citoyen Legrand D'Aussy, Paris, 1803.

CHAPTER IV.

Diplomatic Negotiations and Preparations for War.

1. In October A.D. 1400 Manuel Palæologus, the Emperor of the Greeks, was the guest of Henry IV., the King of England. All the information we can find about that visit is in the old Hakluyt, who quotes Thomas Walsingham's words: "*The Emperor of Constantinople came into England to seeke ayde against the Turks, whom ye king, accompanied with his nobiltie, met withall upon Blackheath upon the day of St Thomas the Apostle, and received him as beseemed so great a prince, and brought him to London and royally entertained him for a long season, defraying the charges of his diet and giving him many honourable presents. And a little afterward the Emperor departed with great joy out of England whom ye King honoured with many precious gifts.*"[1]

The Emperor was the guest of the King, Charles VI., in Paris before he came to England. The French royal historiographer, the anonymous monk of Saint Denis, has left us some more interesting details of the

[1] Hakluyt's *Collections of Early Voyages*, vol. ii. 178.

imperial visitor. He tells us that the Emperor was dressed in robes of white silk, that he rode a white charger, from which he alighted with singular grace when he became aware of the approach of the King of France. " *The Emperor,*" the chronicler continues, "*was a man of middle stature : but his broad chest, his muscular members, his features full of nobility, his long beard and white hair, drew on him the eyes of all the people and made everybody say 'that he is worthy indeed to wear the imperial crown!'* "[1]

This man, whose handsomeness and noble bearing made such a deep impression on the Parisians of A.D. 1400, was the father of Constantine, the last Emperor of the Greeks. His mother, Irene, was the daughter of Constantine Dragasses, or Dragash, who held the north-eastern portion of Macedonia for some time as an independent and afterwards as a vassal-prince of the Sultan. Through her father, Irene was nearly connected with the Serbian royal dynasty of Nemanyich, which was famed for the physical appearance and intellectual gifts of its scions, who boasted to have a strain of the noblest French blood in their veins, brought to them by Princess Helene de Courtenay, who, as Queen of Serbia (1262–1308), exercised great influence on Balkan politics.

As yet no authentic portrait of the last Emperor of the Greeks has been discovered. But as from his

---

[1] *Chronique du Religieux de Saint-Denys, contenant le règne de Charles VI.*, 1380–1422, publié par M. L. Bellaguet, Paris, 1839, p. 757.

handsome and gifted father he inherited the purest of blue blood—that of the Imperial Palæologues—and as from his probably beautiful and certainly most able and virtuous mother he might have inherited the physical and intellectual qualities which were so prominent in the greatest of the Serbian sovereigns—Tzar Stephan Dushan the Mighty—we may readily suppose that his personal appearance was as noble as his life and death were. His contemporary and personal friend, Francisco Philelpho, has given the best description of him when in a letter to the King of France (dated 13th March 1450) he calls Constantine a man "*of pious and elevated mind.*"

Constantine was born on the 9th February 1404, the eighth of the ten children of Manuel Palæologus and Irene Dragasses. All their sons were more or less gifted men; but whilst John, Andronik, Theodore, Demetrius, and Thomas were very ambitious and even selfish, their brother Constantine was simple, honest, unselfish, and straightforward. His brothers distinguished themselves mostly as diplomatists; he was the soldier of the house. When the weakness of the Empire and the confusion of its internal policy were increased by the restless greed of his brothers, he was known to be always endeavouring to make peace between them, and ever ready to give up his own appanages to those who were dissatisfied with theirs. His devotion to the military profession, his earnestness and disinterestedness, as well as his known love for justice, secured for him a decided influence with his family and with the people. So it came to pass that when the Emperor John VII. had, in the autumn of 1437, to leave for the Council of Ferrara (transferred in the next year to Florence), not Theodore, the second brother of the Emperor, but Constantine, a much younger one, was chosen as Regent of the Empire. No doubt this selection was decided by the circumstance that already at that time he enjoyed the reputation of a good soldier, and that it was thought desirable to place at the head of the Government some one who could inspire the people with confidence in the case that the Turks should suddenly attack Constantinople in the absence of the Emperor.

2. Knowing well the insufficiency of the military forces of his own country as well as the superiority of Turkish forces in number and in organization, Constantine was deeply convinced that without military assistance from the Western powers the Greeks would not be able to retain for a longer period even the shadow of their old Empire. With such a conviction he earnestly and sincerely desired the reconciliation of the Greek and Latin Churches. On this point he was decidedly at variance with the majority of the Greek people, and with some of his own brothers. His political notions came into practical play when he came to govern Peloponnesus for the second time as an almost independent ruler. The heir presumptive, Prince Theodoros,

in 1443 suddenly desired to exchange his possessions in Peloponnesus for Selimvria, which was held by Constantine. Constantine, always ready to oblige, met his brother's wish cheerfully, and from 1444 we find him as Despot of Misithra.

Initiated into the preparations for a league of the Christian powers against the Turks, he began at once to organize an army in the Peloponnesus, and to strengthen his defences by raising a wall across the narrow isthmus at Hexamilion.[1] Informed by the Pope that King Vladislaus of Hungary and Poland and the famous Hunyady were on the way to Adrianople, Constantine undertook immediately a diversion, and fell into Northern Greece against the Turkish forces there. He was victorious in several engagements, and was well on the way to clear Achaia altogether from the Turks and subdue to his authority the last French master of Athens, Duke Nerio; but then the news reached him that the Hungarian army was totally defeated by the Turks at Varna (10th November 1444), and he had to withdraw back to Peloponnesus.

The Emperor John and his counsellors were sufficiently astute to escape compromising themselves in the eyes of the Sultan. They neither sent an auxiliary corps to join the Christian army under Hunyady, nor made the slightest effort to prevent the Turkish forces crossing from Asia to Europe. There

[1] *Chalcochondylas*, pp. 319, 342.

was in Constantinople a strong Turcophile party, which often, almost always indeed, succeeded in imposing its programme on the Emperor. This programme consisted in keeping an absolutely passive attitude, so as to avoid provoking the attack of the Sultan. To prove the wisdom of its policy, the Turcophile party could show not only the Hungarian catastrophe at Varna, but also the disastrous consequences which speedily overtook the anti-Turkish policy of the simple, patriotic soldier Constantine. Sultan Murad invaded Greece (autumn 1446), stormed the fortifications at the Isthmus on the 4th of December, and let loose his irregular cavalry over the peninsula, robbing, killing, and destroying. The patriotic Greeks asserted loudly that the battle at Hexamilion was lost only through the treachery of the Albanian volunteers. However that might have been, Constantine was obliged to ask the Sultan for peace, expressing his readiness to accept loyally the position of a vassal and pay yearly tribute. Peace was concluded, and in the spring of 1447 Constantine and his brother Thomas went personally to Thebæ to pay homage to Sultan Murad II.[1]

The people of Morea suffered terribly from the scourge of the Turkish invasion. Not less than 60,000 men and women were carried away as

---

[1] *Phrantzes,* p. 202; *Chalcochondylas,* 345; *Ducas,* 223; *Thrynos,* vs. 78.

slaves. The sufferers laid all the responsibility on Constantine. The Turcophiles of Constantinople were loud in their denunciation of the folly of Constantine's Occidental or Philo-Latine policy. And even those who never for a moment doubted Constantine's patriotic motives and the general soundness of his programme, could not help acknowledging that a strange fatality was the only outcome of his patriotism and wisdom. It is thus that among the superstitious Greeks the impression began to develop that Constantine was apparently a man born under an "unlucky star."[1]

The impression that he was not a "lucky man" must have been strengthened by the misfortunes that occurred to him personally. When in his twenty-fourth year he married Theodora Tocco (1st July 1428), who brought him as dowry the city of Clarentza.[2] But already in November 1429 his wife died, and Constantine remained a widower up to the summer of 1441, when at the instance of his brother, the Emperor John, he married Catharina Gattilusio, niece of Francesco Gattilusio, Prince of Lesbos. But his second wife died suddenly on the island Lemnos in August 1442, while he was with her on the way to Constantinople. In the period between 1444 and 1448 he made several attempts to marry for the third

[1] *Thrynos*, vers. 85–95.
[2] There exists a supposition that the title of the Dukes of Clarence came originally from this city of Clarentza, which luckless Theodora brought to her still more luckless husband Constantine.

time, but neither the negotiations to wed Isabella Orsini del Balzo, the sister of the Prince of Taranto,[1] nor those with the Doge of Venice for the hand of his daughter, were successful. It seems then that he was disposed to marry Anne,[2] the daughter of Lucas Notaras, the Grand Admiral of the Greek Fleet, when also that project had to be abandoned on account of the sudden call of Constantine to higher destinies.

3. The Emperor John VII. died on the 3rd of October 1448. Constantine was now the eldest of the surviving sons of the Emperor Manuel II., and there was not the slightest doubt of his legal right to succeed his brother, the late Emperor. But his younger brother, the restless, ambitious, and unscrupulous Demetrius, happened to be alone at the deathbed of the Emperor John, and his partisans began seriously to consider should they not proclaim Demetrius, and disregard the rights of Constantine. A legal pretext they found in the circumstance that Demetrius was born "in the purple" while his father was a reigning Emperor, whereas Constantine was born before his father ascended the throne. But, independently of that consideration, there were other circumstances which encouraged them. Prince Demetrius was as well known in Constantinople and Adrianople for his Turcophile sympathies as Despot Constantine was for his

---
[1] Hopf, *Geschichte Griechenlands*, ii. 110.
[2] Sathas, *Monumenta Historiæ Hellenicæ*, ix. p. 17.

inclinations towards an alliance with the Latins. And when, a few days after the burial of the late Emperor, the Sultan crushed the Hungarian army under Hunyady at the field of Kossovo (18th October 1448), the chances of the Turcophile Demetrius seemed considerably to overbalance those of the unfortunate friend of the defeated hero of the Christian League. No doubt the Empress Irene, the venerable mother of the Palæologue princes, who still lived and exercised great influence within the circle of her imperial family, advocated decidedly the rights of her son Constantine, to whom she was greatly attached. The influential statesmen, Manuel Cantacuzene, Manuel Jagros, and Lucas Notaras, were also loyally standing for Constantine. So was also Thomas, the youngest of the Palæologue princes, when he reached (on the 13th of November) Constantinople. But the arguments of the Prince Demetrius' partisans were based not so much on personal as on public grounds—the political interest of the State. At last a compromise was made: an embassy was to be sent at once to the Sultan to ask him, Would he acknowledge Despot Constantine as Emperor or not? This course was perhaps the only one to prevent civil war, or eventually an attack on the part of the Turks, but it shows more than anything else the growing weakness of the Empire, and the failing sense of dignity.

Sultan Murad II. was a thoroughly honest and upright man. He hated bad faith, and during his reign the Porte was famed for the scrupulous fulfilment of all engagements. It would have been clearly the political interest of Turkey to raise up discord in Constantinople, or at least to set on the throne a prince who was a tried and proven Turcophile. Yet Sultan Murad did not hesitate to declare that he would at once acknowledge Constantine as Emperor, because the Greek throne belonged by right to him.

Prince Demetrius and his partisans were greatly disappointed, but they had sufficient wisdom to accept the question as definitely settled. In December a special deputation led by old Manuel Jagros left Constantinople for the Peloponnesus, carrying with them the insignia of the imperial dignity. On the day of Epiphany, the 6th of January 1449, Constantine was crowned in Misithra as the Basileus of all the Greeks.

4. He entered Constantinople the 12th of March of the same year, and was warmly received by the citizens.[1] He at once gave proof of his conciliatory disposition. To his brother Prince Thomas he gave the rank of "Despot," the highest after that of the Basileus himself; to Prince Demetrius he ceded Misithra with all the province he lately ruled. Before these two princes left Constantinople they were requested by their mother, the Empress Irene, to

[1] *Phrantzes* says the citizens "exceperunt novum dominum universi benigne et hilariter, impleti exultatione et lætitia, magnosque agentes triumphos," p. 206.

swear solemnly in her presence that they would live in brotherly concord, supporting each other faithfully. It was the last dramatic pageant in which the venerable Empress, perhaps already in the dark robes of the nun Hypomene, was a central figure, surrounded by her three sons, and all the stately splendour of the Byzantine Court. She died soon afterwards, on the 23rd March of 1450; and although Despot Thomas and Prince Demetrius soon forgot their solemn oaths, the Emperor Constantine never ceased to speak of her with the highest respect and affection.

Constantine gave proof of his conciliatory disposition and prudence in yet another way. On his arrival in Constantinople some suggestions were made to him that it would be well to repeat in St Sophia the ceremony of coronation, as otherwise some citizens of the capital might doubt of his being formally anointed Basileus. It was one of those peculiar themes, in which theological and political aspects were so intimately interwoven, the discussion of which was so attractive to the Byzantine mind. But Constantine refused to act on the suggestion. His position was strong from the canonical point of view, as it was clear that the sacrament of anointment performed in the modest church of Misithra was quite as valid as if it had been performed at the splendid altar of St Sophia. His political grounds for refusal were specially mentioned, and are more interesting: a new coronation in Constantinople would give occasion to reopen the strife between the friends of the union with the Latin Church and their opponents. The Emperor wished to see internal peace established, and peace with the Sultan not compromised, and therefore naturally found it wise to avoid reviving the delicate question of the relations of the Eastern Church and the Roman See.

This policy, to avoid anything likely to provoke the Turks, was indicated by the circumstances of the time. Within the last five years the Hungarian armies which had attempted to break the power of the "Grand Turk" had been repulsed by crushing defeats, and the Kingdom of Hungary, the only safe base of operations against the Turks, needed time to reorganize her own forces. And then there could be no serious talk of the formation of the Christian League as long as France and England were at war with each other. This passive and temporising policy—which was followed not only by the late and the new emperors of Constantinople, but also by the Despot George of Serbia—was met cordially by the policy of the Sultan Murad and his Grand Vizier Chalil-Pasha-Tchenderli. To both these statesmen it seemed the paramount interest of the Turkish Empire to gain time to consolidate its position in Europe, to take a firm hold of the extensive territories which they had with such an amazing rapidity conquered, and to secure the subjection of the Balkan nations by the establishment of a strong military and administrative government. This they thought to secure by a policy of moderation and conciliation, which would fill Greeks and Serbs with confidence that no immediate danger menaced them from the Turks, that the *status quo* would be loyally maintained for an indefinite time, and there was therefore no pressing need to push forward the formation of the League of the Christian nations against the Moslem power in Europe.

Under such circumstances the first two years of Constantine's reign passed peaceably. He left the question of the re-union of the Churches as he found it, viz., quietly sleeping, and cultivated friendly relations with the Ottoman Porte and with orthodox Serbia. He did his best to prevent his two restless brothers in Peloponnesus coming to open conflict, and thought again of looking for a consort for himself. His faithful friend Phrantzes had already in October 1449 left Constantinople on a matrimonial mission to the orthodox courts of the kings of Trebizonde and of Iberia.

5. But this idyllic calm could not last long. The honest, but of late years somewhat indolent, Sultan Murad died on the 5th February 1451, and his eldest son, Mohammed II., ascended the throne.[1]

---

[1] I follow the usual English way of writing the name of the conqueror of Constantinople. But from the study of contemporary

The new Sultan, quite a young man, who had not yet completed his twenty-first year, was generally considered incapable and pleasure-loving. This opinion was based on the fact that he had been once before on the throne, but when in 1444 there came a moment of great danger, his own Grand-Vizier Chalil thought it his duty to summon the old Sultan Murad to reassume the reins of government.

Statesmen, however, who were intimately acquainted with men and things at the Ottoman Court—as, for instance, the Serbian prince, Despot George, the Greek minister, Phrantzes, and the envoys of Venice and of the Duke of Milan at the Porte—knew well that Mohammed was a youth of fiery ambition and great personal ability.

Under the influence of his stepmother, Mara Brankovich, one of the most cultured women of her time, and of some Greek renegades at the Turkish Court, Mohammed had acquired a decided taste for reading, greatly appreciating the Greek and Latin works on Alexander the Great, Cyrus, Julius Cæsar, and Theodosius the Great. Mara's part in the education of the heir-apparent was so great, and her civilizing influence so generally admitted, that she was by many contemporary writers assumed to be Mohammed's own mother. But Mohammed had

Serbian and Greek writers there is no doubt that his name was Mehmed or Mahamed.

Pelasgian blood in his veins, being the son of a beautiful Albanian slave.

Mohammed was, in fact, the perfect type of a highly educated Oriental potentate, grown up under influences coming from re-awakening Europe. To his knowledge of languages (he knew Arabic, Greek, Latin, and Slavonic), and to his pronounced predilection for historical works, he joined a great love of Persian poetry, astrology, and occult sciences. He tried his hand at Persian versification, and was deeply interested in astrological interpretations. He was of choleric temperament, and therefore somewhat impulsive. But when political objects were in question, he showed himself a past master in the art of astute dissimulation. As a young man he was deeply religious, but later seems to have joined a body of Turkish free-thinkers, and in their company sometimes made witticisms at the expense of their great Prophet. Full of noble ambition, clever, and of great personal valour, he is justly considered one of the greatest of the Ottoman Turks.

The first acts of the young Sultan were exceedingly conciliatory. He retained Chalil Pasha as Grand-Vizier, indicating therewith his intention to continue his father's policy of keeping up the *status quo*. When the special envoys from the Emperor of Constantinople and the Despot of Serbia arrived with the usual presents and congratulations, Mohammed received them very graciously. He solemnly engaged himself

MOHAMMED II., THE CONQUEROR OF CONSTANTINOPLE.

[*To face p.* 90.

by oath to keep peace with their sovereigns, and to respect faithfully the treaties concluded with them by his father. He assigned to his stepmother, the Sultana Mara, rich estates in Macedonia, and gave her permission to return to her father. To the Greeks he promised to pay yearly 300,000 aspers (10,000 Venetian ducats), that they might keep properly Orchan Effendi, an Ottoman prince, great-grandson of Bayezid Ilderim, who had sought and found refuge in Constantinople. To ensure the payment of that amount certain towns in Macedonia were ordered to pay their taxes direct to receivers appointed by the Greek Emperor. This gave occasion for the eagerly credited rumour that the young Sultan was so anxious to secure the goodwill of his neighbours the Greeks that he had ceded to the Emperor certain parts of Macedonia.

Another proof of this disposition seemed apparent in the Sultan's request that the old Despot George should mediate for a durable peace between the Porte and Hungary. Having sent special plenipotentiaries to Smederevo, the capital of Serbia, the Sultan crossed, in the summer of 1451, to Asia Minor to subdue the rebellion of the restless Ottoman vassal, the Emir of Karamania.

6. Prince George Brankovich of Serbia—or rather "Despot George of Serbia," as he was best known to his Christian contemporaries—was one of the most

remarkable men of his time. Chevalier Brocquière visited him in Serbia A.D. 1433, and speaks with enthusiasm of his venerable appearance, great wealth, and splendid Court.[1] Another of his contemporaries, Francisco Philelpho, in his letters to the Doge of Venice and to the King of France, described George as "one of the most prudent and powerful princes of the age."[2] A third and justly famous contemporary, Aeneas Sylvius Piccollomini (subsequently Pope Pius II.), said of him that "by his personal appearance and in other respects he was full of dignity and deserving of the highest respect, but unfortunately he belonged to the Greek Church!"

Possessing numerous and extensive estates in Hungary, he was a member of the Hungarian House of Lords, and was nearly elected Regent of Hungary instead of John Hunyady (1445). He was considered almost a member of the imperial family of Greece, his first wife, Maria Comnena, having been the daughter of the Emperor Alexius Comnenus of Trebizonda, his second wife being Irene, the daughter of Manuel Cantacuzene, and his son Lazarus having married in 1445 the daughter of the Despot Thomas Palæologus, niece of the Emperor Constantine Dragasses. Despot George exercised considerable

---

[1] *Voyage d'Outre-mer*, p. 130.
[2] F. Philelphi, *Epistolæ*, p. 574 (ed. Paris, 1503).
[3] *Aeneas Sylvius, Europa*, p. 235.

influence at the Porte also, partly through his daughter Mara, whom Sultan Murad II. married in 1436, and partly—probably in a great measure—through his frequent and splendid presents to the Pashas and Viziers of the Sultan. On the ascension of Mohammed II. to the Ottoman throne George Brankovich was the most influential ruler between the Carpathians and the Bosphorus, and it was in acknowledgment of that fact that the Hungarian and Turkish plenipotentiaries met in his capital to negotiate for the peace under his supervision.

In the suite of the Turkish commissioners was a Greek, employed probably as an interpreter. The man seems to have been an ardent patriot, and possessed of real political sagacity. Whenever he had an opportunity of meeting the old Despot George alone, he implored him to prevent the conclusion of the peace, "because," he argued, "if the Sultan secures peace with the Hungarians, he will have a free hand to strike down Constantinople!" Phrantzes recorded this, and added, "but, unfortunately the Despot of Serbia would not so much as turn his head to look at this suggestion, much less was he willing to reason about it!"[1]

It was not likely that the experienced statesman, of whom acute observers like Philelpho and Aeneas Sylvius thought so highly, had not considered all the

[1] *Phrantzes*, iv. c. 2, p. 323.

circumstances. But it seems the privilege of fatality to make the wisest and most logical men foolish in the end, and things the most unforeseen the most certain to be accomplished. In August 1451, when the negotiations in Smederevo were proceeding, there was absolutely nothing to justify the upposition that an attack on Constantinople was imminent. Had not the Sultan given abundant proof of his desire to live in peace with his neighbours? There was no pretext whatever for such an attack, and it was not likely the Greeks would wantonly provoke a quarrel. Moreover, the Sultan had retained for Grand-Vizier Chalil, the old personal friend of Despot George and of the Greek Emperors, a shrewd statesman, who knew very well that to precipitate such an attack would accelerate the formation of the European coalition, and thus eventually bring about the fall of the young Ottoman Empire in Europe, rather than the conquest of the Byzantine capital.

Yet, though all visible signs and all plausible arguments indicated a long period of peace, Despot George, who was essentially a man of compromises, thought it best to allow only a three years' *armistice* to be concluded between the Porte and Hungary, instead of a formal treaty of peace.

7. Amongst the Greek statesmen, and in Constantinople generally, the opinion prevailed that no im-

THE FORT RUMILI-HISSAR (MOHAMMED'S BOGHASI-KESEN).

mediate danger was to be apprehended. The situation looked so pacific and the political sky so cloudless that the only question worthy of attention seemed to be—the marriage of the Emperor.

Constantine was of an age when marriages for love can give place to marriages from more solid considerations. The people expected their twice-widowed Emperor to remarry properly and judiciously. Constantine, looking for a suitable party, after some hints from his relative Protostratorissa Palæologina, aunt to the Sultana Mara, asked himself if, after all, the Sultana, with her family connections and her supposed influence at the Porte, could not bring to the Greek throne considerable political advantages? She was certainly no longer young—Phrantzes deemed her two or three years older than Constantine—but she was still handsome, dignified, highly cultured, and, because of her great charity, highly esteemed by the poor and the clergy. In addition to all this, Mara's father was famed through all the East for his immense wealth, and as the widow of a Sultan and stepmother of the reigning Padishah she was believed to have abundant means of her own. Yet, as often happens with men of the sword who lose courage before the shadow of a woman, Constantine dared not mention his conclusions and his inclinations to any one at his Court. Fortunately, two interesting communications reached him, and made him open his lips,—one from his envoy and friend Phrantzes, the other from Despot George himself.

The letter from Phrantzes would have been interesting enough even if it had contained nothing but a portion of a conversation with the King of Iberia. The King had a daughter of truly Circassian beauty. Phrantzes wished to know the amount of dowry this Princess would bring if the Emperor married her. The King rejoined that, instead of giving money with his daughter, he expected to receive money for her, at which Phrantzes could not suppress his great surprise. "Well," continued the King, who was famed for his extensive knowledge,—"what will you? Every country has its own customs and manners! Look, for instance, at Britain. There *it was usual for a woman to have several husbands at the same time!*"[1]

But there were other matters of interest in the letter. Having arrived at the Court of the Emperor Alexius Comnena of Trebizonde, who had several marriageable daughters, the envoy went one day to the palace for a private audience with the Emperor. Alexius received him with the question: "*What will you give me for a piece of good news?*"—and then informed him that Sultan Murad was dead, and that the new Sultan Mohammed had sent with great honours his stepmother Mara to her father, Despot George. Alexius, being the first cousin to Mara, was

[1] *Phrantzes*, p. 247.

naturally well informed about her movements. Phrantzes instantly forgot the Iberian beauty and the marriageable daughters of Comnena, thinking the most eligible marriage for his master and friend would be one with Mara Brankovich.

Not knowing of Constantine's personal inclination he wrote at some length to convince him of the advantages to accrue from such a union, answering in advance all possible objections. One of these being their near relationship, Phrantzes argued that Mara, having always been so liberal to the Church and the clergy, none could doubt but that the Church would grant at once the necessary dispensation.

The communication from the Despot George was to the same effect. The old man was decidedly ambitious, and would have liked exceedingly to see his daughter Empress of Constantinople. He seems to have offered to Constantine a very rich dowry and other advantages.

Constantine did not longer hesitate. He sent his own relative, Protostrator Manuel Palæologue, to the Court of Serbia, to ask formally for the hand of Mara. Manuel was apparently chosen because he had family connections with the Cantacuzenes, and would therefore be received not merely as a friend, but as a relative, the Serbian Court being presided over with much splendour by Irena Cantacuzena, the comparatively young wife of the old Despot.

But the fabric so laboriously constructed by far-seeing statesmen was blown away by a woman's breath. Mara, favourably known for her delicacy of feeling, good tact, and political foresight, declared with much dignity to her father and to the Emperor's special envoy, that she had vowed to consecrate her remaining life to the service of God, and therefore must decline the hand of the Emperor. Some people thought she did this from consideration for the feelings of her cousin, Anna Notaras, the abandoned *fiancée* of Constantine.[1]

This episode, with its pleasant hopes and final disappointments, was another sign of the peaceful situation in the first months of the Sultan Mohammed's reign.

8. But the confidence arising from the general opinion that no immediate danger threatened them, encouraged the Greeks to venture on a step which suddenly and unexpectedly reversed the whole aspect of affairs.

The Greek finances were in an exceedingly bad condition. There was a large public debt with short terms of repayment, while the revenue of the Empire was small and uncertain. The Treasury was not able to punctually meet the salaries of the State officials and the pay to the few permanent companies of the Emperor's bodyguard. This irregularity and poverty

[1] Sathas, *Monumenta Hist. Hellenic*, ix., Preface.

was the cause that the famous maker of big guns, the Hungarian Orban, left the service of the Emperor and entered that of the Sultan, who gave him at once a salary four times as large as that he should have received from the Greek Government.

Looking at the empty Imperial Treasury, and listening to the reports of the conciliatory disposition of the new Sultan, the Greek statesmen came to the conclusion that they had not sufficiently turned to financial advantage the evident wish of Mohammed to live in peace. Some one made the fatal suggestion that it was not yet too late to mend matters, and that the Sultan's campaign in Caramania was a most favourable opportunity for representing to him that 300,000 aspers were not adequate for the support of an Ottoman Prince with becoming dignity, and still less sufficient to render a dangerous pretender inaccessible to ambitious temptations. It seemed to be a simple and ready method for increasing the Imperial revenue. Special envoys therefore were despatched to the Sultan's headquarters at Broussa, and there received by the Grand-Vizier Chalil-Pasha.

According to Francesco Philelpho, Chalil was the son of a Serbian father and of a Greek mother. He was captured when a child, made a Mussulman, and educated to serve the Ottoman Empire. His policy of wise moderation, yet of great decision when action was needful, had carried the Empire successfully through many crises during the reign of Sultan Murad II. But greed of wealth was his notorious failing, and this, combined with his consequent conciliatory policy towards the Greek and Serbian Courts, aroused suspicions that he was in the pay of the wily Greeks, and of rich old "Vuk-Oglu," as the Turks called Despot George. The impatient military party disliked him for his patience and moderation, while the common people took revenge for his stinginess by nicknaming him "*Gyaour-Yoldash*" and "*Gyaour-Ortagh*" ("the comrade and partner of the infidels").

This old friend of the Greeks was amazed when he heard the object of the Greek embassy. The ambassador apparently thought it would be easier to secure the success of his mission if he hinted that, in the case of a refusal, the Greek Government might, perhaps, cease to restrain the action of Orchan-Effendi. Apparently it was just this hint which aroused the indignation of the aged Grand-Vizier.

"You foolish Greeks!" exclaimed Chalil; "long ago I learned to know your falsehood and your cunning! While Sultan Murad lived it was possible for you to go on comparatively well, because he was just and conscientious. But Sultan Mohammed is quite another man. If Constantinople escapes his impetuosity and his power, it will be a proof that God does not punish your crooked ways and your sins. Fools! The ink on the documents of peace concluded between us has not yet dried, and you come to us with silly threats! You are mistaken. We are not inexperienced and simple children to be easily scared. If you really believe you can do something, you are free to do it! If you desire to proclaim Orchan Sultan of Romania, go and proclaim him! If you wish to bring the Hungarians from across the Danube, call them, and beg them to come! If you desire to recover the countries you have lost, try! Be sure, however, of this one thing: you will only succeed in losing the little that remains your own!"[1]

This answer is so in keeping with the character and general conduct of Chalil, that Ducas, who gives it in his history, might have heard it from the lips of the very ambassadors to whom it was addressed.

The point in this answer is the foreshadowing of the possibility that the destinies of Constantinople would be accomplished before Hungary (or Europe at large) could come to its rescue. That opinion was evidently held by those who surrounded Sultan Mohammed in the summer of 1451. It very quickly deepened and spread, and took active forms.

The Sultan himself received the Greek ambassadors courteously. He, who was so hasty and impetuous, did not show the slightest annoyance when told the

---

[1] *Ducas*, xxxiv. 132.

[2] It was Hammer who first noticed the character of genuineness in Chalil's speech (Hammer, *Geschichte*, i. 504).

object of their mission. On the contrary, he expressed himself quite willing to do anything right and equitable, and would gladly consider their proposals as soon as he returned to Adrianople.

9. In the beginning of the autumn of 1451 the Sultan arrived at his European residence, with ready answer to the Greek demands. Orders were immediately issued to send away the Emperor's receivers from Macedonia, and to suspend payment for Orchan Effendi; Hungarian Orban, the chief of the Turkish cannon foundry, was ordered to hasten production of heavy guns; and, in addition to all these preparations, the Sultan announced his determination of constructing a castle on the European shore of the Bosphorus, facing Fort Anadoli-Hissar on the Asiatic side.

The point selected for the new fortification was on Greek territory, only four or five miles north of Galata, at Loemocopia, where existed the ruins of an old castle and an old church dedicated to the Archangel Michael.[1] According to a legend, Alexander the Great crossed to Asia at this place.

It was without parallel in the history of the world that a sovereign should seize a portion of the territory of a neighbouring State, with which he was at peace, and build himself a fort on it! The news produced intense commotion amongst excitable Greeks of the capital, especially as it was evident to everybody that

[1] *Le Beau*, xxi. 227.

the two forts could cut off at any moment the supplies of corn from the Black Sea!

Chalil endeavoured to maintain some diplomatic courtesy by sending a special envoy to the Emperor, with a polite request for a formal permission to erect the fort on that particular spot. He explained that the Sultan's decision was prompted exclusively by his desire to protect commerce, as the Catalonian corsairs would not venture into the straits when they knew that every ship approaching the line of the Sultan's forts must stop to pay passage dues and show regular papers.[1]

The Emperor and his councillors were in great consternation. The question was how to effectually meet Chalil's diplomacy. They could devise nothing better than the worn-out expedient which had helped them so often. They hoped the shadow of the West, thrown slightly across the Sultan's path, might produce its old effect. Therefore the Turkish envoy received as answer: "That the Emperor would cheerfully oblige his friend the Sultan, but unfortunately the territory in question did not really belong to him, having been ceded long ago to the Franks of Galata, and he therefore feared the building of the fort on Frankish ground might bring the Sultan into collision with Frankistan!"[2]

---

[1] These details have been first recorded by the Janissary Michael, *Povyest Janezara*, p. 173, and are confirmed by Sa'ad-ud-din.

[2] The Turkish historians speak explicitly about the Greek attempt

The Greek diplomatist who prepared this answer doubtless felt proud of his skill. But the experienced statesman who sat on the velvet cushion of the Grand-Vizier "smiled in his beard" at the cleverness of the Greeks. He turned their answer against themselves, saying, "The Sultan, unwilling to hurt the feelings of his good friend the Emperor, did not wish to begin to build without his formal permission; but as the Emperor now declared the ground belonged to the Franks, the Sultan, who does not care a straw for the feelings of the Franks, will without further delay proceed with his fort!"

10. The Greeks were thus entrapped by their own cunning. The Emperor and his councillors were in duty bound to consider carefully the situation. All rumours about the great ambition of the young Sultan, all tales told in the bazaars about Sultan Murad having on his deathbed impressed on his son the duty of conquering Constantinople (Sa'ad-ud-din), all hints the Grand-Vizier threw out concerning the resolute character and probable policy of his new master, were now substantiated by the stern fact that the Sultan was about to construct a fort almost at the very gates of Constantinople. They could not for a moment seriously accept Chalil's proferred explanation of the Sultan's pacific motives, and his desire to protect only

to represent the territory in question as belonging to the Franks, *Sa'ad-ud-din*, 163.

the interests of commerce. They could no longer question what was the ultimate purpose of Mohammed, and they must have felt that this was really the beginning of the end.

All these considerations led only to one conclusion: to the necessity for a change in the foreign policy. The passivity of the Greek Government of the last years, their readiness to leave unfulfilled the decisions of the Florentine Council, their neglect in cultivating closer relations with the Western powers, had been possible only under the condition that the Turks respected the *status quo*. This foundation of their foreign policy was now shattered by a sudden and rude shake of the impatient and grasping hand of the new Sultan. For Constantine and his advisers remained now nothing else but to turn to the West of Europe for aid.[1]

It must have been peculiarly humiliating to Constantine to be obliged now to appeal to the Pope, after having for more than two years ignored the Florentine engagements. He had to explain away the late policy of the Greek Government, and to apologise for the

[1] Mr Stassulyevich (*Ossada i vzyatiye Vizantii Turkami*) has advanced the theory that Constantine was personally responsible for the catastrophe, inasmuch as he wantonly abandoned the "national policy" of his predecessor, and without provocation and necessity sought the alliance with the Latins, which naturally exasperated the peace-loving Mohammed, and forced him to undertake the conquest of Constantinople, so to say, in self-defence against the Western powers. As I see the facts, they are pointing to a quite different conclusion.

neglect and delay in executing engagements so solemnly entered into. The Emperor's letter has not been preserved, but from the Pope's answer it is evident that the Emperor did make some explanation and some apology. The Greek ambassador, Andronicus Briennius Leonardus (or Leontaras), must have been received in Rome about the end of September 1451, as the Pope Nicholas' answer to the Emperor is dated 5th October the same year.

In his answer the Pope reminds the Emperor of the solemnly-proclaimed union in Florence, of which the "witnesses were all the Christian countries," amongst which he mentions also England, Scotland, and Ireland ("testis est Britania, major Anglicorum regis subjecta ditioni, testis Hibernia et Scotia, insulæ maximæ extra continentem positæ"). Only the Greeks seem to ignore the decree of the Union ("tamen apud Graecos Unionis hujusmodi decretum silentio tegitur"). The Pope did not dissimulate the irritation of the Holy See at the conduct of the Greeks. The last sentences of his letter are not only emphatic, but almost menacing:—" If you, with your nobles and the people of Constantinople, are ready to execute the decree of the Union, you will find us and our venerable brethren the Cardinals, together with the whole Occidental Church, always willing to work for your honour and your State; but if you and your people refuse to execute that decree, you will force us to make such provisions as may seem fit to us for your own salvation and for our honour." As a proof of the Emperor's honest intentions, the Pope demanded that the Patriarch Joseph, who had been banished from the patriarchal throne in consequence of his faithful adherence to the Union, should be recalled and reinstated.[1]

With that letter and its categoric declarations Leonardus returned to Constantinople towards the end of the autumn 1451.

11. During the winter of 1451–1452 the Emperor continued his endeavours at the Porte to induce the Sultan to abandon his intentions concerning the fort. But all his representations were of no avail. Mohammed pushed only the more actively his preparations. The best masons were selected from all parts of the Empire, and brought to the shores of the Bosphorus. Building materials were collected, many Christian churches and ruined castles serving as quarries. The Archangel's church in Loemocopia was the first to be pulled down. Several plans for the building of the castle were elaborated, and one in the form of a triangle chosen. As a figure of cabalistic meaning, it was supposed to augur success. Some thought the triangular shape was adopted in honour of the Sultan, the first letter in his name being of the triangular form. Probably simply technical considerations de-

[1] The whole letter printed in Raynaldi, *Annales ecclesiastici*, xviii. 376.

termined the adoption of the plan, as triangular fortifications were popular in that age.

The Sultan left Adrianople on the 26th of March 1452, and timed his journey so as to reach on the *seventh* day the spot selected for the new fort, where five thousand masons were waiting for his arrival. The foundations were immediately laid with great Kurban festivities, rams being slaughtered and their blood freely mixed with the chalk and mortar in the first layers.

When the earliest reports of the commencement of the works reached Constantinople, the Emperor seemed disposed to make a sally, and, sword in hand, stop the proceedings. Constantine Dragasses was in fact rather a simple, honest soldier than a skilful diplomatist. But his councillors prevailed upon him to abandon the idea, and to try a new mission to the Sultan.

New envoys were sent. This time the Greeks spoke plainly, saying: "Should the Sultan persist in raising the fort he would practically break peace with the Greeks, and violate the treaties which his predecessors had kept loyally, and which he himself had confirmed by solemn oath." They declared further that Constantinople could not enjoy peace, nor would peace be of any value to its citizens, as long as starvation, viz., the cutting off of the importation of corn, should hang over their heads, like the sword of Damocles. The Emperor was quite willing to pay a yearly tribute, but he considered it his duty to insist on the Sultan's abandoning the construction of the fort.

It is interesting to find Mohammed bringing forward filial piety as a motive for a political act. He related to the Greek envoys that, eight years ago, when the Hungarian army under King Vladislaus and Hunyady stood at Varna, preparing to march on Adrianople, his father, having experienced great difficulty in crossing from Asia to Europe, made a vow to build a fort on the European side, so as to secure to his army safe crossing and recrossing. Death had prevented his father accomplishing his vow, and it was the son's present duty to fulfil it!" "*Do you think you can prevent me doing it?*" asked the Sultan, in conclusion; "*this ground does not belong to the Emperor, and why should he come in my way? Go and tell your master that I am able to do what my predecessors were not able to do, and that I am willing to do what they would not do! And mark this also, I shall have every ambassador impaled who dares henceforth come to me with such a message!*" [1]

This answer created a panic in the city. Crowds gathered in the markets and other open places; some men appeared stricken down by terror, others eagerly related new versions of the Sultan's answer; some

---

[1] The Christian and Turkish writers are in perfect accord on the general character of Mohammed's answer: *Ducas*, 238; *Cheirrulah*, 58; *Hammer*, i. 505; *Zinkeisen*, i. 315; *Mordtmann*, 12.

struck their breasts, exclaiming: "Here are the last times! Here are the days of Antichrist and of our destruction! What is coming upon us? Better, O Lord, let us die by a pestilence than that our eyes should see the fall of our city, or our ears should hear Thy enemies tauntingly ask, 'Where are now the saints that watch over their town?'"

But there were numbers of men, without families and without home, who looked on with contemptuous smiles when the artisans and shopkeepers hurried to the churches to cross themselves a thousand times and touch the floor with their foreheads hundreds of times. The numerous small inns were filled with men without occupation, who, over bowls of spiced wines, laughed loudly at the fright of the citizens. Of such men, a few companies of volunteers were formed, which on their own account sallied forth through the northern gate to drive away the Sultan and his masons. None of them returned to the city. They were all cut to pieces or taken prisoners by the Turks.

Sa'ad-ud-din relates that the Sultan ordered Mohammed-Bey, the son of Ac-Tchailou, to ravage the immediate neighbourhood of Constantinople, and that this commander captured much cattle, and made prisoners of all the Greeks that he found in the fields outside the city. Possibly it was this Mohammed-Bey who encountered and cut down the Greek volunteers, and who afterwards with his flying column watched the gates of Constantinople.

The same historian mentions that the infidels' confusion was extreme after the Sultan's answer. "They did not know what to do," he adds, "except to send their friend Chalil a present of some big fishes filled with gold." Chalil certainly did his utmost to persuade the Sultan to at least reassure the Emperor by renewing assurances of peaceful intentions. But the Sultan thought it better to leave that suggestion to be considered and decided after their return to Adrianople. It is most likely Chalil gave his advice, not because of the golden fishes, which floated probably only in the imagination of the enemies of the Grand-Vizier, but from political considerations. He knew well that the Emperor's ambassadors had been sent to the European Courts, and that despair sometimes proves to be a source of great strength. As a cautious man, he might have honestly and in good faith advised his master not to push matters to the extreme.

The fort was completely finished after four months of assiduous work. Its walls were 25 feet thick; each of its angles was fortified by a strong and high tower, armed with cannon which could throw balls of granite or basalt of enormous size. Several smaller towers connected those three principal ones.

The Sultan gave the fort the name of "*Boghasi-*

Kesen,"[1] "the fort that cuts off the straits," and placed in it a garrison of 400 Janissaries, under the command of Firhudin-Bey. He then rode with a strong escort towards the walls of Constantinople and reconnoitred its fortifications. On the first of September he reached his residence on the Maritza.

12. The Emperor Constantine was on his side earnestly engaged in preparations for the defence of his capital. He called out volunteers, and purchased provisions and military stores. But these orders were given with some apprehension, the Treasury being almost empty. He despatched letters and agents to his brothers, who reigned in the Peloponnesus, almost as independent sovereigns, requesting them to send troops to assist in the defence of the Byzantine metropolis. No doubt he corresponded in the same sense with George Scanderbeg, the Prince of Albania, with Despot George of Serbia, and Hunyady of Hungary.

His special ambassadors left again Constantinople in January 1452 on their way to Venice and Rome. They were in some degree successful with their mission to the Doge. Venice, being the first naval and commercial power of that age, had great interests at stake in Constantinople and the Levant. Its Government had independent and reliable information about the Sultan's movements and projects, and were

---

[1] Later the fort obtained the name of "Rumili-Hissar," which it bears to this day.

quite accessible to the representation of the Greek ambassadors. They sent at once an order to the Governor of Crete to engage Greek volunteers at the expense of the Venetian Treasury, and forward them to Constantinople. On the 24th of February the Doge Morosini signed letters to Pope Nicholas, to the Emperor Frederick of Germany, to King Alfonso of Sicily, and to Hunyady, the Regent of the kingdom of Hungary. The Doge described to them in gloomy colours the dangerous position of Constantinople, and urged them to send at once help to the menaced city.[1]

Genoa, which possessed the whole of Galata as her own dependency, was also well informed of the dangers of the situation in the East. Her Government, in a letter addressed to King Alfonso of Sicily (written one day in the spring of 1452), told him that two special envoys sent by the citizens of Galata had arrived in Genoa, and brought reliable information that the Sultan would next spring move with great force against Constantinople ("*quod adversus Constantinopolim et Peram Machometus Turcarum Dux in ver proximum summa vi movitur*"). They said they were glad to have just heard that an envoy from the Greek Emperor has reached his (Alfonso's) Court; they informed him that they themselves were making preparations to send, with the opening of the spring,

[1] *Acta Archivi Veneti*, ii. 454.

ships with men and arms to Constantinople, and urged him to do so likewise.[1]

Meanwhile the Greek ambassadors reached Rome. They were honourably received, as they brought positive assurances of the readiness of the Empire to accept formally, honestly, and seriously the Union of the Churches. The Pope and the Cardinals were highly gratified, and set at once to work. Special Legates were sent to all more important European Courts, but the greatest importance was attached to the missions to Paris and to London.

At that time it was the general impression in Europe that if a new crusade against the Turks was to be carried to a successful issue, it must be undertaken and conducted by France. The greatest publicist of the time, the acknowledged European authority on all questions concerning the East, Francesco Philelpho, expressed this opinion very clearly in the memorandum which he addressed to the King of France on the 13th of March 1450. He urged the King to undertake the task because he was the only sovereign in Europe who could do it, and because all the Christian world expected that he would do it. He discussed the arguments which the King might bring forward as an excuse, and of which the only serious one was—that the hostility of England prevented him doing what otherwise he would gladly

---

[1] Raynaldi, *Annales Ecclesiastici*, ix. 605.

undertake. "But it is not at all likely," continues Philelpho, "that Englishmen would prevent you entering upon such a sacred enterprise; the English are a religious people, and it is more probable that they will be ready to follow you, after the example of their forefathers, who always followed the French kings and assisted them whenever these moved against the infidels."[1]

Philippe, Duke of Burgundy, who was considered the champion of the Eastern Christians, did his best to induce the King of France to put himself at the head of the movement to save Constantinople. The moment he got, in 1451, the information (most likely through letters from the Emperor Constantine) of the changed situation at the Bosphorus, he sent Sire Jean de Croy and the Chevalier Jacques de Lalaing as his special envoys to King Charles, and invited him to combine with him and the King of Sicily to save Constantinople.[2]

Now in the beginning of 1452, shortly after Constantine's new embassy made satisfactory declara-

[1] "Nec est tibi praeterea subverendum ne quid adversum te tumultus in Francia aut in regnique tuo Gallia per Anglos insurgat cum exercitum adversus infideles eduxeris, nam necque ipsi Angli ullo modo patientur ut sunt homines religioni dediti, sed tam piae, tam sanctae, tam gloriosae expeditionis expertes duci, sed positis et prostratis cunctis simultatibus propter Christum alacres te sequuntur, imitati scilicet majores suos, &c.":—Philelphi ad Gallum Regem adhortatio, *Epistolae*, ii. 12.

[2] Barante, *Histoire des Ducs de Bourgogne*, vii. 5.

tions in Rome (at the end of January or the beginning of February), the Pope sent Cardinal d'Estoutteville to the King of France, and the Archbishop of Ravenna to King Henry of England, with the instructions to invite them to make peace and jointly turn their arms to support Constantinople against the Turks. The King of France declared himself quite willing to make peace with England and hasten to assist the Emperor of the Greeks. But King Henry's answer to the Pope's Legate was to the effect, "that of peace they could only speak at some future day when the English had reconquered by arms all the places they had lost in France."[1] Cardinal d'Estoutteville remained in France, at the request of King Charles, to conduct the new investigation into the case of the Maid of Orleans, but the Archbishop of Ravenna returned from England, "having lost all hope of seeing peace concluded" ("Spe pacis sublata abcessisse").

The results of these important missions were very disappointing. The Pope must have seen the possibility of being left alone to help. As an honest man he declared at once to the Greek ambassadors that, though in the worst case he will assist the Emperor alone, his help cannot be great, and will not go beyond sending a few ships with men and money. He advised the ambassadors to go themselves to visit the more important Courts of Europe, and impress upon

[1] Raynaldi, *Annales Ecclesiastici*, xviii. 575.

them the necessity of forwarding assistance to Constantinople, promising to lend them cordial support in their task.

The ambassadors, acting upon this advice, visited several Courts in Italy, and went to Paris, "*everywhere with tears in their eyes praying for help,*" as Pope Nicholas relates himself in his last will. But after all they had to return to Rome without practical results, having been only met with kind words and promises that "*what should prove possible would be done.*" Aeneas Sylvius, speaking of these efforts of Pope Nicholas and the Greek Emperor, wrote: "*To our shame be it said: the ears of our princes were deaf and their eyes blind!*"[1]

The same year the Emperor Frederick came to Rome to be solemnly crowned as "Roman Emperor." He had already received letters from the Emperor Constantine asking aid, also letters from the Doge of Venice and from Pope Nicholas, setting forth the necessity of some common action. In Rome he found the atmosphere of the Vatican impregnated with Greek lamentations and Catholic ambitions. The Pope and the Roman Emperor thought it desirable to make at least some sort of demonstration of their good-will. A conference of all the Cardinals present in Rome was held under the presidency of the Pope, to hear Bishop Aeneas Sylvius make, in the name of the

[1] Raynaldi, *Annales Ecclesiastici*, xviii. 414.

Emperor Frederick, certain declarations. Sylvius, one of the most brilliant orators of the time, described vividly the great sufferings and misfortunes the Christians had endured since the arrival of the Turks in Europe. He spoke strongly of the indifference and coldness of the European princes, who looked on unmoved while the Mohammedan power grew strong at the expense of the Christians. "*Unfortunately*," he said, "*the Saracens* (so he called the Turks) *are far more ardent in their infidelity than we are zealous in our faith. We look on violence done to Christians and remain quiet; our religion is trampled down and in danger to be put under the yoke, yet we only turn our eyes on the other side!*"

At the conclusion of the address Sylvius declared that the Emperor Frederick had firmly resolved to lead his armies against the Turks, but of course relied upon the powerful support of the Pope, whose word could unite all the faithful "*in this holy enterprise*," and secure its ultimate success.[1]

The Pope gave his blessing, but his answer was not quite satisfactory. He said personally he did not desire anything more fervently than to see an earnest crusade undertaken against the Turks; but before making any promises binding on the Holy See, he must first inform himself of the desires and intentions of other Christian Courts.

---

[1] The whole speech in Raynaldi, *Annales*, xviii. 590–593.

After the conference Frederick returned to Vienna, and seemed very soon to have forgotten everything that was promised in his name at Rome.

The Greek ambassadors, losing hope of any serious support from the Western powers, begged the Pope to send at least the help he had himself pledged to them. The Pope replied that he was willing to act when the union of the two Churches was finally accomplished, and the Patriarch of Constantinople and the Greek clergy had solemnly acknowledged the papal supremacy.

The poor Greeks declared themselves ready to accept all the conditions if the Pope would only send men and money for the defence of their capital. Thereupon Cardinal Isidore was appointed Papal Legate, with a special mission to Constantinople.

Isidore was a Greek by nationality. Many learned Greeks and Serbians of the fifteenth century went to Russia to make for themselves a career. Isidore, by his erudition and energy, had succeeded in placing on his head the mitre of Archbishop and Metropolitan of Moscow. Being actually the most learned Russian prelate, he was sent as representative of the Russian Church to the Council of Florence. There he subscribed to the Union of the Churches. But both the Russian Church and the Russian Court repudiated his action, and he was obliged to leave Russia and seek refuge in Rome. He was received there with great honours, promoted to the dignity of a Cardinal, and a most important and delicate mission was now entrusted to him.

On his way to the Greek capital, the Cardinal stopped at several islands in the Archipelago, and called for volunteers to enrol themselves under the Papal banner. But he was not very successful. Only a few volunteers joined him (some say not more than fifty!), and with them he arrived in Constantinople at the beginning of November 1452.

There he found the position very sad and gloomy. Commerce had been completely paralysed by the recent events, and by the general feeling of an impending catastrophe. The people were without work, and almost without bread. They were in constant alarm in consequence of the continually recurring rumours of the appearance of Turkish irregular cavalry, who plundered and burnt the farmhouses, and destroyed the crops under the very walls of Constantinople. Everyone felt that, without early and efficient assistance from the West, the capital must fall a prey to the overwhelming power of the Turks; yet the majority of the citizens were full of bitterness and hatred against everything Latin. The lower orders of priests, monks, and nuns (and Constantinople was crowded with them) thought it a less evil that the Sultan should take up his abode in the Old Imperial Palace, and St Sophia be transformed into a mosque, than that the name of the Pope should be pronounced there in public prayers. And many of them did not believe the danger of Turkish conquest was so imminent. Some who pretended to great learning brought out and circulated among the populace an old prediction, that the residence of the Emperors would not pass to other masters until ships were seen sailing under full canvas across the dry land—which, in plain language, meant *never*. Why then should the people, flying from an imaginary danger, fall into the embrace of Antichrist?

But the Court, the majority of the nobles and statesmen, as well as a certain number of the higher clergy, knew better. The Emperor and the new Patriarch Gregorius signed the declaration accepting the Union of the Churches, with the express reserve, that after the present peril had past, all the points of the compact between the Churches should undergo new and careful revision with the view to a definite settlement. This reserve was the small safety-valve which supplied the oppressed consciences of the Patriarch and clergy, and perhaps of the Emperor himself, with a breath of air.

On the 12th of December a solemn *Te Deum* was celebrated in St Sophia. Cardinal Isidore and Patriarch Gregorius officiated together, in the presence of the Emperor and his Court, and " *Many years to Pope Nicholas* " was chanted, with the accompaniment of suppressed sighs and tears.

14. Meanwhile the populace, headed by monks and priests, ran through the streets, hurling anathemas at the betrayers of their Church and the Empire, and expressing in every possible way their utter disgust and abhorrence of the ceremony then going on in St Sophia. Some one mentioned the name of Gennadius. Thousands immediately echoed it, and great masses of people rushed to the monastery of Pantocrator.

The monk Gennadius—otherwise known by his secular name of Gregorius Scholarius—was at one time a senator, and famous for learning and patriotism. It was he who gave a curious interpretation to an inscription on the tomb of Constantine the Great, declaring it to be a prediction of the conquest of Constantinople by the Turks. Gennadius accompanied the Emperor John to the Council of Florence, and there deeply impressed the Latin doctors by his erudition. He signed there the Church Union, but having returned to Constantinople, cursed his own deed, resigned his offices, and withdrew from the world. As "Father Gennadius" he lived in the cloister of Pantocrator, from whence he directed the agitation against the reconciliation with Rome.

And now, on this 12th of December, dense crowds of people gathered around the walls, and pressed against the gates of that famous monastery, calling upon Gennadius with impatient voices to direct them in this emergency. He had the courage on the 15th

November to speak from the pulpit, in the presence of the Emperor and his Court, against the Union. Now he did not personally appear, but caused a written declaration to be nailed on the gate of the monastery. People pressed eagerly to read the words which were written: —" O you Greeks, worthy of all pity! Where have your errors carried you? You are unfaithful to your God, placing your hope only on the help of the Franks, and with your city you give also your faith to ruin! May God be merciful to me! I do not carry your shame on my soul! Unhappy ones, stop a moment and consider what you do! With your city you lose the faith your fathers have left you, and go over to infidelity! Woe to you on the Day of Judgment!"[1]

This written answer of Gennadius was like oil on flames. The excited people left the place more angry and miserable than when they arrived there. Some of the more moderate citizens ventured to observe that, after all, without the help of the Latins, the city would be captured by the Turks; but the mob shouted angrily: "*Better we should be Turks than Latins!*"

The addresses given by a Bohemian that day at several places in the city greatly increased the excitement of the people. He had been Catholic, and had later turned a follower of John Huss. He told the

---

[1] *Ducas*, 141; *Leonardo*, 257; *Ubert. Pusculus*, vers. 477–488. *Genadius*' Memorandum to the Emperor against the Union, in P. Migne's *Patrologiæ Cursus*, vol. clx., where are also his manifestoes to the citizens, dated 27th November and 12th December.

crowds who thronged to hear him all sorts of stories about the evil practices of the Popes, each story more absurd and disgusting than the other.[1]

It was generally known that the Minister of State, Kyr Lucas Notaras, the Great Admiral of the Fleet, and a relative of the Emperor, was decidedly opposed to the Union. He had not only refused to assist at the ceremony in St Sophia, but loudly spoke to every one who chose to listen, that he preferred far more to see in Constantinople the turban of a Turk than the helmet of a Latin.[2]

All this produced a painful impression upon the Emperor Constantine. He heard the curses heaped upon him at the very moment when he was sacrificing his own personal feeling to save, if possible, the ancient Empire. He did not attempt to suppress the disorders by military force, but permitted the unfortunate people to cry themselves hoarse. When worn out with their own violence, the crowds grew still, and a sullen quietness reigned throughout Constantinople almost more unbearable than the wildest clamours.

After the 12th of December a melancholy solitude settled down upon the splendid church of St Sophia, as scarcely any one went into it to pray. Most of the so-called "everlasting lights" burning before some of the relics and of the "miraculous eikons," were extinguished long before the arrival of the Turkish Imams.

---

[1] *Ubert. Pusculus*, vers. 531-558.   [2] *Ducas, loc. cit.*

Even the name of St Sophia provoked impatience and indignation among the ignorant and fanatic Greeks, who now considered the church " nothing better than a Jewish synagogue or a heathen temple." None would receive communion from the hands of the priests who had officiated in the church on the day of the Union, nor were they allowed to bury the dead or baptize children. Especially much hysterical excitement seems to have prevailed among the nuns. One of them, highly esteemed for her piety and learning, declared " *she would not fast any more; she would eat meat, wear Turkish garments, and offer sacrifices to Mahomet!*" The excitement and the hatred against the Catholics became so intense, " *that*," as Ducas says, " *even if an angel from heaven had descended, and declared that he would save the city from the Turks, if only the people would unite with the Church of Rome, the Greeks would have refused!*"[1]

This deplorable state of things was aggravated by the want of patriotism and political wisdom displayed by the nobility and the higher classes in general. The difficult position in which the Emperor Constantine was placed cannot be better described than in his own words. In November of 1451, he wrote to his friend Phrantzes:—" If I except thee, there is no man here with whom I can hold counsel; every one looks solely after his own private interests; since thou

[1] *Ducas*, 257.

hast gone abroad my mother has died, and shortly after her died also Cantacuzen, who was capable of impartial judgment; Lucas Notaras asserts loudly that he alone knows what ought to be done, and that nothing is good and wise except his own words and deeds. The great Domesticos is angry against the Serbians, and goes hand in hand with John Cantacuzen. With whom, then, can I take counsel? With the monks? or with men who are as ignorant as they? With the nobles? Every one of them belongs to one party or another, and would betray to others the secret I might confide to him!"[1]

15. However, in the midst of all these troubles and anxieties Constantine did not forget the duty of preparing as well as possible for the defence of his capital. Provisions of all sorts, especially corn and oil, were collected into the State magazines; all the princes and independent rulers, near and distant, were appealed to for military assistance; special commissioners were appointed to repair the city walls, and conscription made of all men fit for military service. As the Treasury became exhausted, and as the appeal to the patriotism of the higher classes proved of little avail,[2] the Emperor, on the advice of his Synklytos, or Privy Council, ordered that churches and monasteries should

[1] *Phrantzes*, 222.
[2] "El povero Imperador cum lachrime domandava prestasseno danari per condur provisonati ; et quelli inravono esser poveri, disfatti, che dapoi presi il Signor Turcho quelli trovo richissimi."—*Dolfin*, 22.

deliver up to the imperial mint their gold and silver, to be coined for the use of the State, and gave them in exchange receipts engaging to repay them fourfold when the peril menacing the city had passed away.[1]

All this while Constantine continued in Adrianople his diplomatic endeavours to avert the danger. Chalil-Pasha, though compelled to be doubly careful and cautious on account of the increasing influence of the war party, worked continually, and in his own way, for peace. Despot George Brankovich was doing the same.

But all these influences were unavailing. The idea of capturing Constantinople had taken complete possession of the mind of the Sultan. From boyhood an admirer of the great conquerors, he was filled with ambition to immortalize his name by a notable conquest. He clung to this idea with religious fervour, and this very likely gave some foundation for the popular version that his father Murad, when dying, had commended to him the conquest of Constantinople as his last desire.[2] The exhaustion of the natural allies of the Greek Empire—the Serbians and Hungarians—the confusion in Peloponnesus and in Albania, echoes of wars between France and England, perhaps also the knowledge that the Pontifical Chair in Rome was occupied by an old man—who preferred to collect books and bind them beautifully, to undertaking the

[1] *Phrantzes*, 256.   [2] *Sa'ad-ud-din*.

terrible anxiety involved in the organization of a new crusade—all these gave fresh encouragement to Mohammed's ambitious plans. He consulted astrologers, and what they told him, and what he read himself from the stars, only contributed to hurry him onward. But he consulted also much with experienced men of war, discussed with them the plans of campaign, and himself drew up sketches of the proposed dispositions of his army.

He was occupied with this question day and night, and became quite sleepless, so intent was he upon devising the best means for capturing the ancient yet never old, world-famed residence of the Cæsars. On one occasion about midnight he sent for Chalil-Pasha. The old Grand-Vizier through all his long career had never yet been disturbed at such an unusual hour. Even a man with a perfectly clear conscience might well have felt uncertain whether he was not called to encounter the rage of the impulsive Sultan, whose ear was not always closed to intriguers and calumniators. Chalil appeared before the Sultan, carrying above his head a bowl filled with golden coins. Mohammed was sitting on his bed, completely dressed. When he saw his grey-bearded Vizier enter bearing the bowl after the fashion of slaves, he asked, "*What does this mean, my Lala (my uncle)?*" "*Sire,*" answered Chalil, "*it is an old custom that dignitaries of state, when the Padishah calls for them at unusual hours, should not appear before his Majesty with empty hands!*" "*Put that away!*" said the Sultan; "*I do not want your gold; what I want you to do is to help me to capture Constantinople!*"

The Vizier judiciously cast himself into the current of his master's thoughts, and said that for himself he doubted not that God, who had made the Sultan lord of all the provinces of the Greek Empire, would deliver to him also the capital of that Empire. Chalil added that he was ready to sacrifice his life and everything else in his master's service.

The Sultan replied: "*Look on this my bed! I turn on it all night, from one side to the other. I wish only to remind thee that thou must not allow thyself to be softened by gold or silver. Let us, with a firm will and with persistence, fight the Greeks, and trusting in God and his great Prophet, let us work to win the residence of the Cæsars!*"[1]

Possibly soon after this peculiar conversation an official communication on the part of the Sultan was sent to the Emperor. We do not know its nature, but the text of the Emperor's answer has been preserved.

"*As it is clear*," wrote Constantine to Mohammed, "*that thou desirest more war than peace, as I cannot satisfy thee either by my protestations of sincerity, or by my readiness to swear allegiance, so let it be according to*

[1] *Ducas*, 140.

thy desire. I turn now and look alone to God. Should it be His will that the city be thine, where is he who can oppose His will? If He should inspire thee with a desire for peace, I shall be only too happy. However, I release thee from all thy oaths and treaties with me, and, closing the gates of my capital, I will defend my people to the last drop of my blood! Reign in happiness until the All-just, the Supreme Judge, calls us both before His judgment seat!"[1]

There is a remarkable simplicity and quiet dignity in this letter. It breathes the spirit of a brave soldier, a devoted Christian, and an Emperor deeply conscious of his duty to his people and to his own name.

[1] *Ducas*, 141.

CHAPTER V.

MILITARY ARRANGEMENTS OF THE BESIEGERS AND OF THE BESIEGED.

THE last letter of the Emperor Constantine to the Sultan conveys the impression of its being an answer to a formal ultimatum.

The date of the actual declaration of war has not been preserved. From certain expressions of Kyr Lucas, which we shall mention hereafter, it would seem that the war was held to have begun in December 1452. Certainly both parties were openly preparing for it during the winter months.

Experiments with the monster cannon of the age constructed by Urban were made early in the beginning of 1453, to the great satisfaction of the Sultan. He named it "Basilica." Karadja-Bey was ordered to proceed with a corps of 10,000 irregular cavalry to escort the huge gun to the walls of Constantinople. This expedition started one day in February, and required not less than six weeks to reach its destination. The cannon was drawn by 60 yoke of oxen, 200 men marched on each side to support it, while a company of pioneers and sappers levelled roads and made bridges. Karadja's flying corps was meanwhile scouring the country around Constantinople. It is especially mentioned by the chroniclers that on this occasion the castle of San Stefano was taken by storm and sacked.

Armed bands, led by Timar and Ziyamet Beys, the chiefs of the numerous military fiefs, were assembling on the plains around Adrianople during the first weeks of March. The Sultan held a grand review of his troops in the second half of that month. On this occasion the most popular Ulemas, Sheiks, and the white-robed descendants of the Prophet, offered up prayers in the midst of the army for the successful issue of the campaign.[1]

On Friday, the 23rd of March, Mohammed himself left Adrianople with 12,000 Janissaries and several thousand Spahis, his best troops.

The plans for the siege had been leisurely arranged, and perfected in all their details. Every commander knew the exact spot he was to occupy before the walls of Constantinople. A small corps was detached to keep Selimbria in check, and to prevent its garrison and people sending help to the capital. Turachan-Pasha had a large army in Thessaly, holding in check both Scanderbeg in Albania and the Emperor's brothers in the Peloponnesus. To prevent the latter

[1] *Sa'ad-ud-din*, 56.

more effectually from sending assistance to Constantinople, Turachan despatched his son Ahmed with a corps on a raid into the Peloponnesus, and several severe engagements were fought during the summer of 1453 between Ahmed and Mathæas Assan, the Commander of the troops of Prince Demetrius.[1]

Towards the end of March a corps of 1500 cuirassiers was seen riding one day on the road leading from Philippopolis to Adrianople. This was the auxiliary corps which George Prince of Serbia was by treaty engaged to furnish to the Sultan. The men were under the command of a famous captain, Voyvode Yaksha of Breznik. Not even their commander knew exactly their destination. Rumours were current that the Sultan would cross to Asia to put down the rebels of Caramania. When the cuirassiers reached a village on the other side of Philippopolis, a messenger from the Sultan's headquarters met them with an order to take the shortest route to Constantinople, and there join the Ottoman army!

Michael Konstantinovich, who was himself with the auxiliary corps, describes the indignation which this order produced amongst the Serbian officers.[2] Their first impulse was not to proceed further, but to return to Serbia. After some reflection, however, Voyvode Yaksha found that such an action

---
[1] *Phrantzes*, p. 235. [2] *Michael the Janissary*, p. 102.

might injure the interests of his Prince and country. Besides, some friendly Christians in the neighbourhood informed him confidentially that the Turkish garrisons in the towns through which his corps would have to pass on its way back had been ordered not to allow it to return. There remained nothing but to resume the march to the Sultan's camp under the walls of Constantinople.

On the 6th of April the Sultan and his suite arrived at a spot one Italian mile distant from Constantinople. The towers and the domes of the great city were plainly visible. As a true Mussulman, Mohammed ordered first that his carpet should be unrolled, and he turned towards Mecca and prostrated himself in prayer. Rising, he sent "tellals" (public criers) to proclaim through the entire camp: The siege of the city had now begun! Ulemas were ordered to visit each regiment, to incite the "true believers" to go cheerfully to the work, as the Prophet had plainly promised that this renowned and wealthy town should be theirs.[1]

At daybreak of the 7th of April the lines were drawn nearer the town, and each commander led his troops to the position previously assigned them.

The Sultan's tent was pitched on the eastern slope of a small hill, now known as Mal-Teppé, lying somewhat to the right of the gate of St Roman.

[1] *Sa'ad-ud-din*, 157.

In front and on both sides of the Sultan's tent were placed the Janissaries, and in front of these, directly opposite to the St Roman's gate, the great "Basilica" and three other enormous guns were formed into a formidable battery.

On fourteen other points batteries of four ordinary cannon were erected. Nine of these batteries were strengthened by one additional and heavier piece, so that 56 ordinary and 12 great cannon, besides "The Basilica," making altogether 69 cannon, were placed in positions against the land walls of Constantinople. No contemporary power could show anything approaching this formidable artillery of the Sultan in magnitude.[1]

These batteries were ready by the 11th of April. This, considering the circumstances, speaks well for the skill of the engineers and the energy of the commanders of the Ottoman artillery.

Besides the cannon, which represented the most modern weapon of the time, there were placed between the batteries some of the old catapults, which threw large stones against the walls and into the town. In the Turkish History "*Tatch-ul-Tevarrih*" it is stated: "Stones thrown by the catapults and arbalets carried before the Eternal Judge the enemies who defended the forts and towers of Stamboul."[2]

---

[1] *Phrantzes, Ducas, Barbaro, Dolfino,* and others.
[2] *Ahmed-Djevad Bey, Etat Militaire Ottoman,* i. 205.

And the use of these antiquated machines is also mentioned by Giacomo Tedardi, who was one of the volunteer defenders of the city.[1]

The right wing of the Turkish position was occupied by troops levied in Asia Minor, under the command of Mustapha-Pasha, the Anadoly Beyler Bey. The left wing was composed of troops levied in the Balkan Peninsula and commanded by the Rumili Beyler Bey Turachan. Behind the centre of the position was placed a strong reserve. On the other side of the Golden Horn, Zagan-Pasha and Karadja-Bey occupied a hill and a field, which at that time formed the common of Galata, and on which the suburb of Pera was afterwards built. Zagan and Karadja kept the Italian suburb of Galata in check, and their battery at the top of the hill commanded the western portion of the Golden Horn.

No previous Ottoman Sultan had marshalled so numerous an army as the one brought together by Mohammed under the walls of Constantinople. Eyewitnesses and contemporaries disagree about its numerical strength: Chalcochondylas estimated it at 400,000 men; Archbishop Leonardo at 300,000; Ducas says it had 265,000 men, Phrantzes 258,000, the author of *Thrynos* 217,000 (adding, however, that of true Turks there were not more than 70,000), Evliya-Chelebi says that the spoil of Constantinople was divided

[1] *Informacion*, 22.

amongst 170,000 warriors; the Venetian Barbaro calculated the number of fighting men at 160,000; the Florentine Tedardi at 200,000, but he explained that of these "*only* 140,000 *were effective soldiers, while the remainder were tailors, pastry-cooks, artizans, petty traders, and other men who followed the army in hope of profit or plunder.*" The Turkish historian Cheirrulah says the besieging army had not more than 80,000 fighting men.

Most probably Mohammed brought with him an army of about 70,000, but this army, as the siege proceeded, was increased by thousands of men like those of whom Tetardi speaks.

We are indebted to the same observant Italian for a few features of the general appearance of this Turkish army. His sketch, taken from the very walls of Constantinople, coincides in many respects with what we have already quoted from the Chevalier Brocquière. "*About the fourth part of the Turkish army,*" says Tedardi, "*was armed by haubergeons and jackes; some men were armed in the French, some in the Hungarian fashion, others in various ways; some had iron helmets, others bows and cranquins; some were without other arms than wooden shields and scimitars, a peculiar form of Turkish swords.*"[1]

One of the most important statements which Tedardi made is that the Turkish army contained numbers of

[1] *Informacion*, 21.

Christians of Greece and other countries.[1] The anonymous author of the *Thrynos* gives us even the precise number—*thirty thousand!* This sad detail receives confirmation from the Archbishop of Chios. "*But who has in fact besieged the city,*" he asked himself, "*and who has taught the Turks the military art, if not the Christians themselves? I have seen with my own eyes that the Greeks, the Latins, the Germans, the Hungarians, and men of every other Christian nationality were mixed up with the Turks, and with them together stormed the walls!*"[2]

This fact conclusively shows the moral confusion then prevalent amongst the Christians in the Balkan Peninsula, and it is doubly sad when compared with the state of things which prevailed in Constantinople itself.

The Emperor Constantine had exhausted every effort to obtain reinforcements, and to place the capital in the best possible state of defence. The Pope began to bestir himself only after he received the report from his Legate that the Union had been formally and solemnly proclaimed. But the representations which he sent to other powers had not much practical effect. Only Venice and Alfonso, the King of Naples, decided to equip each ten galleys to join the other ten warships which the Pope promised to supply at his own expense. But much time was lost in equipping this fleet. Not till the 27th of April, after the siege had been in progress

[1] *Informacion*, 25.   [2] *Leonardo da Scio, La Presa*, 258.

for three weeks, did the Pope sign letters formally empowering Jacob, the Archbishop of Ragusa, to take charge of the equipment of the promised galleys.[1] On the 7th of May the Venetian squadron sailed from Venice.[2] More time elapsed before the fleets united, and they did not arrive at the island Euboea till the second day after Constantinople had fallen!

The repairs of the walls of the city had been unfortunately placed under the superintendence of two monks, skilled in engineering, but greedy and dishonest. It was believed that some of the money, destined for the fortifications, went into the monks' pockets. However that may be, the condition of the walls when the Turks appeared was so bad that the Greeks were afraid to place heavy cannon upon them!

The outside wall had been repaired by the Emperor John Palæologus some time between 1433 and 1444. The inner and higher wall, connecting on the land side not less than 112 square towers, had not been thoroughly repaired for centuries. Most of these 112 towers had been constructed in the ninth and tenth centuries. The walls and the towers along the Golden Horn all dated from the time of the Emperor Theophilus (A.D. 829–841).[3]

On one of the towers on the side of the Sea of Marmara (between Koum-Kapou and Yeni-Kapou)

---

[1] *Raynaldi, Annales Eccles.*, xviii. 610.
[2] *Acta Archivi Veneti*, ii. 454.   [3] *Mordtmann*, 32.

a Greek inscription in bricks remains to this day, showing that that particular tower and the wall adjoining it were rebuilt in the year 1448 at the expense of the Despot of Serbia, George Brankovich.[1] What a terrible irony of fate, to find only five years later, the same Christian Prince assisting the Sultan with a contingent of cuirassiers to take Constantinople!

Dolphin mentions that the tower Anemandra, near the gate called Kylo-Porta, had been repaired by Cardinal Isidore, probably with funds furnished by the Pope.[2]

According to Tedardi's statement, the inner wall was about 20 yards high, the outer being somewhat lower.[3] Measurements made in our time have shown the ditch to have been 40 yards wide.[4]

The weakest point in the walls was considered to be behind the Palace of Hebdomon (near the Egri-Kapoussi of to-day), where there was only a single wall without any ditch. At the request of the Emperor the Venetian captain Alois Diedo set the men from his ships to dig a ditch there. The work was inaugurated on the 14th of March with much ceremony in the presence of the Emperor and of the State dignitaries. On the 31st of March the work was completed. The Diedo ditch was 104 yards long, its scarp being 15 and counter-scarp 13 English feet deep.

---

[1] The whole text of the inscription in the *Miklosich, Monumenta Serbica*, p. 146, and in Mordtmann's *Belagerung*, in the Notes, p. 132.
[2] *Dolphin*, 24.   [3] *Informacion* 23.   [4] *Mordtmann*, 35.

At that time it was known that the Turkish army was approaching, and on the same day, the 31st of March, the Emperor himself mounted guard with his men on a neighbouring hill to prevent Turkish horsemen suddenly appearing and attacking the workmen in the ditch.

The Emperor had ordered a conscription to be made of men able to fight, and of all sorts of arms. Phrantzes, who was charged with this task, reports that he found only 4973 Greeks and about 2000 foreigners capable of defending the walls.[1] Archbishop Leonardo says that there were altogether 6000 Greeks and 3000 Latin Volunteers to defend the city. Tedardi states that there were between 25,000 and 30,000 men capable of bearing arms, but only between 6000 and 7000 combatants. His statement confirms remarkably that of Phrantzes. With a hastily-collected and hardly-exercised force of seven, or, at most, nine thousand men the Emperor Constantine had to defend the weak walls of his capital against an army fully ten times that number, and possessing 69 cannon! And while scarcely *nine thousand* Christians could be found to defend the key of three continents, the glorious residence of the old rulers of the world, thirty thousand Christians were in the ranks of the Sultan's army, ready to shed their blood to bring down the Cross from St Sophia and replace it by the Crescent!

The unhappy Emperor, notwithstanding his personal

[1] *Phrantzes*, p. 241.

and moral courage, was exceedingly discouraged by the results of the conscription. In order to avert a general panic at the very beginning of the defence, he directed that the particulars of the conscription should be kept secret, and at the same time ordered that all ships, of whatever nationality, entering the harbour, should be detained, and if need be their crews compelled to defend the walls. When told that a few nobles and other people had left the town, the Emperor "said nothing, but sighed deeply"[1]

In the great council of war, under the presidency of the Emperor, which had to decide on the final arrangements for the defence, the first and most important question was: To whom should be entrusted the position of St Roman's Gate ? The Turks had placed their heaviest cannon and their best soldiers opposite that gate, and it was obvious that they intended to concentrate their fiercest attack on that point.

When the Emperor raised the question none of the Greek and Latin captains present seemed willing to break silence or to offer any suggestion. Then suddenly Juan Giustiniani di Longo, a Genoese captain who had arrived with 500 volunteers—well-armed Italian crossbowmen—in January, rose, and bowing to the Emperor, said : " *Trusting in God's help, I am ready to stand there with my men, and to the honour of Christ's name defend the gate against the attacks of the enemy !* "

[1] *Phrantzes*, p. 241.

These simple and noble words were greeted by loud cheers from all present.[1] The Emperor thanked the speaker, and promised to bestow on him the island of Lesbos, with the dignity of a prince, if only the Turks should be repulsed.

The Emperor further decided to make his own headquarters in the Church of St Roman, which was in the immediate neighbourhood of the gate, and at that place of greatest danger and honour took under his command 3000 of the best Greek and Latin soldiers.

To the right from the gate of St Roman, in a northerly direction, was the gate called Charsias.[2] There the Emperor posted a small company of Greeks, under command of the famous archer Theodore of Karystos.[3]

The next gate was that of Polyandrium or Milyandrium, now called Edirne Capoussi. The defence of this position was undertaken by the three Genoese brothers, Paolo, Antonio, and Troylo Bocciardi, with a small company of their countrymen.[4]

From this gate the walls extended somewhat to the east towards the Golden Horn, protecting the part of the city called Blaquerna, after the imperial palace

---

[1] *Turco-Graecia*, l. i., p. 9 ; quoted by Raynaldi, *Annales*, xviii. 406.

[2] Earlier writers place the gate of Charsias somewhat more to the north ; but Mordtmann's researches in Constantinople have proved their mistake.—*Mordtmann*, 46 and 137.

[3] *Phrantzes*, 257.   [4] *Barbaro*, 19.

which stood there. That position had been entrusted to the Venetian Baylo (Minister-Resident) Girolamo Minnoti, who commanded a corps formed of Venetian residents and strangers.[1]

Further to the north the walls had no ditch to defend them. This position was called Calligaria, from the name of the adjoining suburb. It was expected that the Turks would here try to make a breach by undermining the walls. With a view to this, the Emperor entrusted the defence to a German mining engineer, Johannes Grant by name.[2]

The command at the north-western angle of the fortifications, at the gate called Cynegion (now Ayvan-Seray-Kapoussi) was entrusted to the Pope's Legate, Cardinal Isidore.[3]

From the central position at St Roman to the left was stationed a small company of Venetians, under the command of their countryman Dolphino. After the conquest, the gate of this position was walled up, and even its name has been forgotten.

Near that gate was the one called Sylivria or Pygi (now Silivri-Kapoussi), which obtained for its commander the learned Greek mathematician Theophilo Palæologue, assisted by the Genoese Mauricio Cattaneo and the Venetian Niccolo Mocenigo.[4]

At the next gate—its name has not been preserved

---

[1] *Barbaro*, 19; *Phrantzes*, 252; *Ducas*, 203.   [2] *Phrantzes*, 254.
[3] *Barbaro*, 17; *Phrantzes*, 253.   [4] *Barbaro*, 16; *Phrantzes*, 253.

—the command was in the hands of the Venetian Fabrucio Cornero.

The south-western angle of the fortifications was occupied by a strong tower, or rather a castle, called Cyclobyon (now the well-known Seven Towers, Yedi-Kuleler). The entrance to this tower was generally called "The Golden Gate," and it was the last gate to the south in the walls stretching from the Golden Horn to the Sea of Marmara. This position was confided to the Venetian N. Contarini and to the Genoese Emanuelo N., who had under their command 200 Italian archers.[1]

It has not been recorded who had charge of the position between the Cyclobyon and the next gate of Hypsomathia. It is supposed that a number of young monks had been collected from the monasteries of the city and stationed at this point, against which no serious attack could have been expected.

Giacomo Contarini, with a small company of his Venetian countrymen, held the gate called Contoscalium (now Koum-Kapoussi).[2]

The next gate was named, on account of its proximity to the church of St Sophia, Chodegetria, and also Basilika (now Ashir-Kapoussi). The command of the position between Contoscalium and Chodegetria was given to the Spanish Consul, Don Pedro Giuliano.[3]

---

[1] *Phrantzes, Barbaro, loc. cit.*
[2] *Phrantzes, loc. cit.*
[3] *Phrantzes,* 252.

Chodegetria was the most eastern gate in the walls washed by the sea of Marmara.

In the Acropolis—now the Eski-Seray, or the Old Seraglio—was posted the ill-fated pretender to the Ottoman throne, Orkhan-Effendi, with a small number of his Turkish followers.

All the positions from the Acropolis to the Cynegion, along the Golden Horn, were placed under the supreme command of Kyr Lucas Notaras, the Grand-Admiral, who not only had the highest military rank in the Byzantine Empire, but was generally considered a brave and experienced officer, though he was not much liked on account of his hasty temper.

At the entrance of the harbour stood a tower in which the Venetian Gabriello Treviso posted himself with fifty men.

A strong iron chain was stretched across the mouth of the harbour. A portion of this chain has been preserved in the Arsenal of Constantinople. It was formed of huge oblong rings of oak enclosed in iron sheets and linked together by small iron rings.

Along that chain, inside the harbour, 15 galleys and a number of smaller craft were drawn up in several lines, and placed under the orders of the Venetian captain, Antonio Diedo. There were in the harbour altogether 26 galleys: 5 of them Genoese, 5 Venetian,

3 Cretan, 1 Anconitan, 1 Spanish, and 1 French, while the remaining 10 were Greek.[1]

Nearer to the centre of the town, in the free space surrounding the Church of the Holy Apostles (where now stands the mosque of the Sultan Mohammed Fethi), was stationed a corps of about 700 men, mostly recruited from the monks, as a reserve force under the command of Demetrius Cantacuzene, and of his son-in-law Nicephoras Palæologus.[2]

All the corps at the walls had priests and monks attached to them for the purpose of constantly saying masses and offering special prayers.

In all the churches day and night services were to be performed almost without ceasing. The morning liturgies were generally concluded by processions through the streets and along the walls.

The Emperor Constantine usually assisted at matins in the church which happened to be nearest as he made his early morning visits to the walls, and often was at the solemn services between morning and noon. Between these devotions and after them, mounted on his Arabian mare,[3] followed by a small but chosen retinue, he made the round of the fortifications, visiting all the positions, impressing on the soldiers "*the duty of enduring everything for God's glory.*" He would

---

[1] *Phrantzes*, 250.   [2] *Phrantzes*, 255.
[3] According to the popular tradition. *Recueil de Chansons Populaires Grecques*, Paris, p. 74.

return to his headquarters behind the gate of St Roman, and after a short rest under a great tent start again on his tour of inspection. In this self-imposed task the Emperor was usually accompanied by his friend Phrantzes and by a distant cousin, the Spaniard Don Francesco di Toledo (the great-great-uncle of the Duke of Alba).

The suburb Galata, on the other side of the Golden Horn, in itself a fortified town, was mainly inhabited by Genoese. They formed a special community under a Syndic, were independent of the Emperor's jurisdiction, and in intimate connection with their great mother-republic. The Galata citizens were mostly avaricious merchants, not caring much for any considerations of public morality or higher policy, but looking always to secure the utmost possible benefits for themselves exclusively. The Greeks heartily detested them as Catholics, arrogant foreigners, and unscrupulous competitors in commerce; and the Genoese fully returned this enmity.

Having heard from their compatriots in Adrianople of the Sultan's extensive preparations, the Galata Genoese thought it quite compatible with their duty towards their fellow-Christians on the one hand, and their duty towards themselves on the other, to act energetically in two directions. They sent to Genoa pressing reports of the danger menacing Constantinople, and advised that military assistance should be promptly despatched to the Emperor. One result of these efforts was the most welcome arrival of their compatriot Giustiniani, with his Italian cross-bowmen. But at the same time they despatched special envoys to Adrianople to impress upon the Sublime Porte the fact that Galata was independent of the Emperor. They offered to pledge themselves to be neutral spectators, and not to assist the Emperor in any way, but demanded that the Sultan should acknowledge their neutrality, and engage not to molest their town. To this the Sultan gladly acceded, and before he moved against Constantinople he promised solemnly to respect the neutrality of Galata.[1]

In consequence of these transactions, while the Greek capital was in the throes of the deadly struggle, Galata remained tranquil, its inhabitants taking the opportunity to make large profits by supplying both belligerents with provisions and other merchandise at exorbitant prices.

Under such peculiar circumstances did the siege of Constantinople take place.

[1] The Janissary Michael gives another version. He says that it was arranged that the Galata people should be unmolested during the struggle; but if the Sultan conquered the city, they should at once acknowledge themselves his subjects.

CHAPTER VI.

THE DIARIES OF THE SIEGE.

THE *Journal* kept by Niccolo Barbaro, a Venetian who fought on the side of the Greeks, the *Memoirs* of the Emperor's friend and constant attendant Phrantzes, the report submitted to the Pope by another defender of the city, Leonardo, the Archbishop of Chios, and the *Slavonic Diary*, written most probably by an eye-witness—these together afford sufficient materials for the reconstruction of the story of the struggle as it proceeded from day to day.

The Turkish cannonade commenced on the 11th of April.

The signal was given by the first shot from the giant "Basilica." It seemed as though a sudden peal of thunder shook the earth and tore the skies, so deafening the crash and far and wide its reverberations. Since the creation of the world nothing like it had been heard on the shores of the Bosphorus. In the city not only terrified women with their children, but men also, rushed from their houses into the street, striking their breasts and exclaiming, "*Kyrie Eleysson! what is going to happen now?*"

They were not reassured when exaggerated reports about the enormous size of the Turkish stone-balls quickly passed from mouth to mouth throughout the city. The Greek cannon (called ἐλεβόλει, helepoli) of the largest calibre threw balls not exceeding one and a half " Kentenar," or 150 Greek pounds. The smallest Turkish balls thrown against the walls were not less than 200 Greek pounds in weight; most of them varied between 200 and 500 pounds, while the Turkish battery in front of the gate of St Roman was throwing balls varying in weight from 800 to 1200 pounds. Fortunately much time was required to clean and reload, so that, even when the Turks loaded with the greatest quickness, these huge cannon could be fired only seven times a day.

On the 12th of April, about one o'clock in the afternoon, the Turkish fleet appeared in sight of Constantinople. It did not undertake anything. The ships dropped anchor near the Asiatic shore, opposite the Diplokynion of that time (now known as Beshiktash). The fleet was not so imposing by the greatness of its galleys as by the number of smaller ships. From the tops of some towers in Constantinople the watchers believed they had counted about 145 bigger and smaller ships composing the Sultan's fleet.

Between the 12th and 18th of April nothing specially noteworthy happened. The cannonade went on day by day. But it had hardly any effect. The Turks did not understand how to point their cannon efficiently. They were also obliged to repair Urban's giant "Basilica," which on the first or second day got out of order. It is specially mentioned that Urban strengthened its resistance to the charge by binding it with several iron rings.

The Greeks endeavoured to lessen the effect of the great stone shot by pouring a mortar prepared with chalk and brick dust down the walls.

Both parties discharged arrows and fired long and heavy rifles. These rifles were as yet rare, and neither Turks nor Greeks had a great number of them. Still, as Barbaro expressly mentions, the Greeks had more of them than the Turks. Most of the riflemen were posted at the gate of St Roman, where, as already stated, the choicest troops were gathered under the command of Giustiniani, to fight under the eyes of the Emperor.

Though the first eight days of the siege were not interesting from a military point of view, they were not without interest of a different kind.

Shortly after the opening of the cannonade the ambassadors from John Hunyady, the Regent of Hungary, arrived in the Turkish camp. With respectful greetings to the mighty "Grand-Turk,"

Hunyady informed the Sublime Porte that he had ceased to be "*Gubernator Regni Hungariae*," and had surrendered all power and government into the hands of the young King Vladislaus. Desiring to restore full liberty of action to the new king, he returned the document signed by the Sultan's Thougra, approving of the armistice concluded in Smederevo 1451, and asked that the document signed by his own—(Hunyady's)—signature might be returned to him.

This was evidently a diplomatic move in aid of the Greeks. Its purpose was to intimidate the Sultan by hinting that the Hungarian army might eventually march against him. It was a move to strengthen the arguments of Chalil-Pasha for peace. Hunyady himself was more of a burly soldier than a diplomatist. This fine diplomatic scheme could have been evolved only in the head of an Italian Cardinal, or in the experienced and versatile brain of the old Despot of Serbia, who was generally considered an extremely skilful diplomatist as well as an able soldier. As it has been seen, the Despot George, at the request of the new Sultan, and against the warnings of a Greek patriot, had mediated successfully for a three years' armistice between Hungary and Turkey. Most likely the anger of Kyr Lucas Notaras and of Cantacuzene against the Despot—of which we have heard from the Emperor's letter to Phrantzes—had been provoked by his intervention in this armistice. If it were true that the armistice had given the Sultan a free hand to attack Constantinople, the cancelling of the same might be considered likely to induce the Sultan to desist from the siege.

But every measure undertaken by George Brankovich, however skilfully and logically planned, almost invariably missed its purpose, and produced unexpected and undesirable results. Once, in a memorable conversation with the famous Franciscan monk John Capistran, George himself said: "*God gave me wisdom but no good luck, and my people will remember me as a wise but unfortunate Prince!*" His people certainly had that opinion of him, and even generally believed his misfortunes were the Divine punishment for the treason which his father, Vuk Brankovich, was supposed to have committed against Tzar Lazar in the great battle on the field of Kossovo, A.D. 1389.

If fatality could constitute a sure mark whereby to recognize the work of George Brankovich, this Hungarian mission to the Sultan's camp was his work. The ambassadors were allowed to visit the great battery in front of St Roman's Gate. When the Hungarian officers saw how the Turks fired their cannon, they laughed loudly, and told them that notwithstanding the weight of their balls they would never succeed in making a breach in the walls. And then these Christians, who came to draw away the Sultan from the walls of Constantinople, actually instructed the

Turkish artillery officers how to level their cannon effectively against these very walls! All the more important contemporary writers relate this fact.[1] Phrantzes gives an explanation which seems to have circulated among the people in the city. He says that the Hungarians really desired Constantinople to fall as soon as possible, as a Serbian hermit, famous for his gift of prophecy, had told Hunyady that Christendom would not get rid of the Turks until they had taken possession of Constantinople!

On the 18th of April the cannonade continued the whole day as usual, intermingled with shots from the rifles and cross-bows whenever and wherever an enemy exposed himself. It was a fine day. The shades of evening descended softly, and the full moon threw her pale light upon the wondrous beauty of the Bosphorus. About nine o'clock suddenly big drums, cymbals, horns, and pipes (zournés) echoed through the Turkish camp along the whole line, and masses of Turkish warriors advanced with loud shouts towards the walls.

In the city at this hour vigils were being held in most churches, and crowds of people filled the naves and outside courts, holding lighted tapers in their hands, often throwing themselves on their knees in prayer at signals given from the altar. The beautiful

---

[1] *Phrantzes*, 239; *Ducas*, 275; *Chalcochondylas*, 448; *N. Barbaro*, 21.

evening had tempted many people into the streets. Suddenly the alarm-signal was sounded from the walls, and the bells from all churches and monasteries began immediately to ring clamorously. The congregations in the churches rushed out terrified, and dispersed in confusion. The Slavonic chronicler, describing this scene, says: "*The reports of rifles, the ringing of bells, the clashing of arms, the cries of fighting men, the shrieks of women and wailing of children, produced such a noise, that it seemed as if the earth trembled. Clouds of smoke fell upon the city and the camp, and the combatants at last could not see each other.*"[1]

The struggle lasted for some time after midnight. Barbaro wrote down in his *Journal* that the Emperor greatly feared the enemy would succeed in forcing an entrance. But the Turks relinquished the attempt, and retired to their camp, leaving many killed and wounded in the moat and on the glacis. About three o'clock in the morning quietness again reigned, broken only by the cries of the wounded for water or for help.

The defenders of the walls were so exhausted by the fight that the Emperor, visiting all the positions before dawn, found in several places the sentinels and guards sleeping heavily.[2]

On the 19th of April the Turks removed their wounded from the glacis, then they carried away and

[1] *The Slavonic Chronicler*, p. 27.   [2] *Ibid.*

burned the bodies of their dead. According to the Slavonic chronicler, the burning of the killed soldiers was a regular practice of the Turks during this siege.

In Constantinople a solemn Te Deum for the Divine assistance in the repulse of the assault was celebrated.

After the church service the Emperor held a council with the principal commanders and some civil State dignitaries. Some of these thought that the assault of the previous night had something to do with the Hungarian cancelling of the armistice, and that the Sultan might raise the siege. To facilitate such a decision it was thought wise to build a golden bridge for him, to enable him to retrace his steps with honour. It was therefore resolved to send an embassy to the Sultan, and to ask for peace on any conditions he might prescribe short of the surrender of the city.

On the 20th of April, about ten o'clock in the morning, four sailing-ships appeared on the southern horizon, and speedily approached Constantinople. One of them was soon recognized as belonging to the Emperor's fleet, and the three others were Genoese trading ships. They were all loaded with wheat bought by the Emperor for the public stores.

Shortly afterwards the whole Turkish fleet was seen sailing to meet them. In the sight of the Greeks and Latins, who crowded the southern walls, the first naval engagement of the Turks with the Christians was fought on this memorable day. A part of the right wing of the Turkish army also witnessed the engagement. The Sultan himself rode forth, with a splendid retinue of Viziers and Pashas, to the shore of the Sea of Marmara, drawing bridle only when the waves began to wash the hoofs of his horse.

The four Christian ships accepted battle with the Turkish fleet of 145 ships. Crowds of people on the walls naturally trembled for what seemed to them the inevitable doom of their friends.

But the Greek and Genoese crews were born sailors. They used their Greek fire so skilfully that in a short time it became evident that great confusion prevailed among the Turkish fleet. The Sultan was dismayed at the aspect the fight assumed, and when his fleet turned back and sailed towards the Diplokynion, he could not restrain his anger. He shook his fist at the cowards, cursed Balta-Oglou, his Admiral, and in a perfect fury spurred his charger into the sea.

But all this demonstration was of no avail. Balta-Oglou took his ships back to their anchoring-place, and the Christian ships sailed on until they dropped their anchors under the city walls, to the great joy of the citizens. Late in the evening the chain which closed the harbour was lowered, two galleys, under the command of the Venetian captains Gabrielo Trevisani and Zacharia Grioti, sailed out, and with a continual flourish of trumpets brought into harbour the four ships, whose captains and crews had done

THE FIRST NAVAL BATTLE OF THE TURKS (AFTER A GERMAN DRAWING OF THE XVII. CENTURY).

[*To face p.* 158.

such honour that day to their compatriots. The captain of the Emperor's ship was Flantanelas, and the names of the three Genoese captains were Cataneo, Novara, and Balanere.[1]

On the 21st of April, under heavy and continued fire from the great Turkish battery, one of the towers defending the gate of St Roman suddenly collapsed. Barbaro, who was himself on that spot, wrote in his *Journal* that had the Turks immediately stormed with only 10,000 men they could have entered the town, and the conquest would have then been accomplished.[2]

Fortunately the Turks, not expecting such an immediate effect of their fire, had made no preparations for a speedy assault. It happened also that the Sultan was not in his usual place on the Mal-Tepé Hill. He had gone very early in the morning with 10,000 horsemen to Diplokyonion. There he called before him Suleyman-Bey Balta-Oglou, the ill-fated Admiral of his fleet, reproached him violently for the disgrace of the previous day, and ordered him to be taken away from his presence, to be impaled, and die a slow and terrible death.

This horrible sentence shocked the Viziers, Pashas, and other state and court dignitaries who were

[1] The description of this naval engagement is given in Barbaro's *Journal*, 24; *Phrantzes*, 248; *Ducas*, 268; . *Chalcochondylas*, 450. Phrantzes adds that the Turks themselves affirmed they lost on that day 12,000 men, which is no doubt a great exaggeration.

[2] *N. Barbaro*, 26.

present into pity, and they fell on the ground before the Sultan, imploring his mercy for Suleyman-Bey. Mohammed was softened, and replaced the first sentence with a second one: in the sight of the whole fleet, of which he had been until that morning the chief commander, and in the sight of the horsemen who accompanied the Sultan, Balta-Oglou received one hundred lashes, one accidentally destroying one of his eyes. His property was also to be confiscated, and the proceeds of its sale to be divided amongst the Janissaries.

After this painful scene the Sultan presided over a great military council specially convoked at Diplokynion. The embassy from the Emperor Constantine had arrived the preceding day, and now the question placed before the Council was: Should the propositions of the Emperor concerning peace be accepted or rejected?

The Grand-Vizier Chalil strongly argued that this opportunity should be seized to withdraw honourably from before the walls. He stated that the assault of the 18th of April, and the naval engagement of the previous day, proved clearly it was not so easy to capture Constantinople, and that while none could foretell the length of the siege, all knew the longer it lasted the greater was the danger that a Christian army might appear in their rear. He reminded all those present that Hungary had already reclaimed its liberty of action, that preparations were progressing in Italy, and that the Venetian fleet might arrive any day. His conviction was that Constantinople would fall into the lap of the Sultan one day, as the ripe fruit falls from the tree, but he (Chalil) thought that golden fruit not yet ripe. His proposal was to conclude peace with the Emperor on conditions which would drain the vital forces from Constantinople, and thereby accelerate the ripening of the fruit, and to that purpose he suggested the demand of 70,000 ducats as the yearly tribute of the Emperor to the Padishah.

According to Sa'ad-ud-din, Sheikh Ak-Shemzeddin-Effendi, the learned Ulema Ahmed-Kurani and Zagan-Pasha, earnestly opposed the arguments of Chalil. It was hardly to be expected the military commanders would vote at this special juncture for peace. It therefore was not surprising that an overwhelming majority of the Council declared for the continuation of the siege.

The answer given to the Emperor's ambassadors was to the effect that peace could be concluded only on the Emperor's immediate surrender of the city. In that case the Sultan would cede the entire Peloponnesus to the Emperor, and guarantee to him undisturbed peace and sovereignty in that State, while to the Emperor's brothers, Demetrius and Thomas, compensation could be given elsewhere.

The arguments of the Grand-Vizier only succeeded in convincing the military commanders that it was imperative to hasten the conquest. As yet the city had been attacked only on one side, and therefore, however small the garrison, it was possible for the Greeks to concentrate their whole force to repulse the assault. It was clear that the chances of success would be infinitely increased if the city were simultaneously attacked on two sides.

As his military advisers seemed to be at a loss for practical suggestions, the Sultan laid before them a plan he had been studying for some time, and for eventual execution of which he had made preparations. He drew attention to the fact that from the shores of the Bosphorus, at a point between Diplokynion and Galata, a valley opened in a south-western direction, skirting the western base of the hill overlooking Galata, and descending gently to the basin of the Golden Horn, and that it might be possible to transport ships from the Bosphorus through that valley into the harbour! The whole distance was not above five English miles.

It is difficult to say whether this idea was an original one with Mohammed. Barbaro says expressly that the Sultan got it from a Christian ("*li fu insegna da un Christian*"). Archbishop Leonardo believes that some one had related to the Sultan what the Venetians had done fourteen years before, when they transported by land their ships from Etch into the lake of Garda.[1]

However this may have been, the Sultan was persuaded of the feasibility of the operation, and gave orders for its immediate execution.

Several thousand men speedily cleared the valley from bush and underwood. A narrow canal was dug through the whole length of the valley, and paved with strong beams, abundantly smeared with tar, tallow, and lard bought in large quantities from the Genoese tradesmen of Galata. Over the greased beams rollers were placed, and on this a small ship to try the experiment. Drawn by buffaloes, and supported and pushed by soldiers, the ship glided along more easily than was expected.

The Sultan ordered that all the ships to be thus transported should have their sails unfurled and their flags hoisted, and that on each vessel bands of music should play martial airs. The Janissary Michael reports that all the batteries kept up an incessant cannonade that night. This detail explains why the Greeks, and especially why the fleet in the Golden Horn, did not prevent the gliding of the Turkish ships into the harbour. The constant fire from Zagan-Pasha's battery on the hill above Galata was sufficient to prevent any ship from approaching the place where the improvised canal entered the Golden Horn.

[1] *Leonardo*, 269.

In the night between the 21st and 22nd of April the Turks had succeeded in thus transporting into the bay of the Golden Horn some thirty ships.[1]

Giustiniani and his men were busy that night repairing the shattered tower at the gate of St Roman, closing the breach with barrels filled with earth and lashed together. The work was well done, and they awaited the dawning day with some confidence.

The citizens of Constantinople, especially the tradesmen and artizans, were early risers. With the first dawn of the 22nd of April the news spread that the Turkish fleet was in the bay! People left their work and rushed to the walls along the Golden Horn, and saw a number of Turkish ships lying in the Galata corner of the bay, under the shelter of Zagan-Pasha's battery. Many a citizen, who had until then hoped against hope, lost all heart that day. But the Emperor did not yet despair. He was mostly troubled by the necessity of sending more men to the north-eastern wall to guard against an eventual attack from that side.

23rd April.—The cannonade on the land side went on as usual without any specially new feature.

The Venetian naval captains met on the galley of Antonio Diedo to consult about the ways and means

---

[1] I follow here the statement of the Janissary Michael. Cheirrulah says there were only 20 ships, while Barbaro speaks of 72, Chalcochondylas of 70, and Ducas of 80.

of destroying the Turkish ships in the bay. This object was the more pressing, as on that day the Turks began to construct a floating battery, or, as some thought, a pontoon-bridge across the bay. After long consultation, the proposition of Captain Giacomo Koko, to attack and burn the Turkish ships at night, was accepted.

24*th April.*—The cannonade lasted with some briskness all day.

The Turks made progress in the construction of what now seemed more distinctly to be a pontoon-bridge. They used empty barrels, binding them together with strong iron chains.

Captain Koko prepared two ships for the night expedition. He covered their sides with bales of cotton and wool, hoping therewith to deaden the effect of the Turkish cannon.

At midnight the sea captains met on Diedo's ship to fix the final details of the expedition. The preparations were nearly complete, and some of the captains pressed for an immediate attack. To this conference some Genoese captains had been admitted, and they requested that the attempt should be put off until the next night, in order that they also might join in it. The rejection of this request would have exposed the Venetians to the reproach that even in hours of great and common danger they could not forego their old jealousy of the Genoese, their old competitors in commerce and naval power. The suggestions were therefore accepted and the expedition postponed.

In the days of the 25th, 26th, and 27th of April nothing remarkable occurred. The intermittent cannonade and the desultory shooting from bows and rifles were continued.

The Turks succeeded in making smaller or larger breaches at various points; these the Greeks and Latins quickly and effectively repaired. But it was already apparent that the defenders were getting each day more and more exhausted. The Turkish archers and sharp-shooters placed in the first line were daily changed and replaced by fresh men from the camp, but the riflemen and archers on the walls could not be replaced.

In addition to this discouraging fact, disquieting rumours of the scarcity of food began to circulate in the last days of April.

The preparations for the naval expedition were continued and completed. But the Genoese seemed not to have conducted their work with necessary discretion. A certain Faiuzzo, finding out the object of the unusual activity on some of the Genoese ships, went over to the Turkish camp, and betrayed the plans of the Venetian captains. A number of experienced artillery men with four cannons were immediately sent to the Turkish ships in the bay, and the utmost vigilance was enjoined on their captains.

28th of April.—Two hours before the dawn of that day a small squadron left its position near the harbour chain, and moved noiselessly towards the western corner of the bay. It consisted of two great galleys of Gabrielo Trevisani and Zacharia Griotti, and three smaller ships commanded by Silvestro Trevisani, Girolamo Morosini, and Giacomo Koko. Two other small ships were taken in tow, laden with gunpowder, Greek fire, tar, and other combustibles.

It had been arranged that the two great galleys, padded outside with bales of cotton and wool, should precede and shelter the others. But the impatient Koko let his ship glide rapidly ahead and took the lead. A few minutes later all the cannon from the Turkish ships were fired, Koko's ship was struck and speedily sunk, Koko and his crew swimming for their lives.

Trevisani's galley moved rapidly onward through clouds of smoke, but was received with a fresh volley, staggered, and sunk. Trevisani and most of his men saved their lives by swimming. The other captains thereupon retired slowly, throwing volleys of Greek fire. But only one of the Turkish ships caught fire and was burnt.

Some of those who tried to save their lives by swimming, in the confusion of the catastrophe swam right to the shore in the possession of the Turks. Being made prisoners, they were the next day beheaded in sight of the soldiers and crowds of people on the walls. This cruelty aroused the indignation of the citizens and the Government of Constantinople to the highest pitch. Unfortunately there were some 260 Turks in the prisons of the city. They were all brought out on the walls, and in sight of the Turkish army beheaded. Phrantzes himself relates this barbarous act of retaliation.[1]

29th of April.—After the excitement of the previous day, this day passed in comparative quietness both in the Turkish camp and in the city.

The expedition of the Venetians which had miscarried was naturally still the topic of all the talk among the Greeks and Latins. The Venetians, who lost about 90 of their chosen sailors and soldiers, felt the loss deeply, and openly and bitterly charged the Genoese with treason. The Genoese retorted that the Venetian ignorance and Koko's foolishness had caused the failure. The mutual accusations turned speedily into mutual menaces, and, as even the Venetian and Genoese volunteers on the walls were on the point of fighting among themselves, the Emperor assembled the commanders and officers of both the nations, and said to them: "*I pray you, my brethren, be of one mind and work together. Is it not enough of misery that we have to fight against such fearful odds outside the walls? For God's sake*

[1] *Phrantzes,* 257.

let us not have any conflicts amongst ourselves within the walls!" [1]

30th of April.— The Slavonic chronicler has noted down that on this day the first discharge from the Turkish giant cannon against the St Roman's position *"shook very much the wall, which was old and somewhat low; the second discharge at noon carried away the upper part of the wall, making a breach five feet wide; the third discharge was not fired because the night came on before the Turks were ready."* [2]

1st of May.—According to the same chronicler, the Turks concentrated the fire from several cannon of ordinary size against the place where the breach had been effected the previous day, but which Giustiniani had during the night filled in "with wood and earth."

"When they had," the chronicler goes on, "in that way worn out the wall sufficiently, then they pointed and fired their great cannon. But the ball went somewhat too high, and struck the wall of the nearest church behind, shattering it into powder. At noon the Turks were just at the point of firing their second shot, when Giustiniani by a ball from his own cannon struck the Turkish great gun and dismounted it. The Sultan, seeing what had happened, cried out in a rage, '*Yagma! Yagma!*' the whole army repeated

---
[1] *Phrantzes*, 258.
[2] *Slavonic Chronicler*, 11.

the shout '*Yagma! Yagma!*' and soldiers rushed towards the wall and filled the moat."[1]

In the city the alarm-bells were rung at once. The Emperor, coming in haste, encouraged men to hold out resolutely. The Slavonic chronicler describes at some length the struggle which ensued, and which was finished by the Turks retreating from the walls after darkness had set in.

Several other witnesses speak of the fight of that day (Phrantzes, Barbaro, Leonardo), differing somewhat as to its commencement, but not essentially. According to them, some of the soldiers were accustomed to leave their places at noon and go home to dine with their families. On this 1st day of May a greater number than usual went away for this purpose. The Turks, seeing but few men on the walls at St Roman's Gate, descended into the moat, and began to pull down with long hooks the fascines and baskets filled with earth with which the breach had been hastily repaired; and thereupon ensued the fight.

Giustiniani complained to the Emperor of this state of things.

2nd of May.—Nothing specially noteworthy happened. The usual exchange of shots.

The Emperor, however, in consequence of what had happened on the previous day, brought the Greek

---

[1] *Slavonic Chronicler*, 12. "Yagma! yagma!" the Turkish call to storm.

soldiers together, and reproached them for exposing the city to the danger of being captured by surprise while they left their places on the walls to go to dine. Many Greeks replied that they were obliged to go away, as neither they themselves nor their families at home had anything to eat. This statement throws a sad light on the want of proper organization, and on the sufferings which the people had already begun to endure.

The Emperor, shocked at this statement, ordered immediately that henceforth certain men, unable to fight, should carry food and drink to those on the walls, and that the families, whose bread-winners were engaged in defence of the city, should be provided with food by the Government.[1] The Commander of the reserve, Demetrius Cantacuzene, was at the same time ordered to inspect the positions several times a day, to ascertain that all the men were at their posts. He also received instruction to search the houses for men who, though capable of bearing arms, hid themselves, to escape the duty of defending the Emperor, the Empire, and their own homes. These cowards were ripe for Turkish slavery. But it seems that there were not a few people in the city who disapproved of every attempt at defence, and loudly abused the Emperor. The Emperor's friend Phrantzes has himself introduced these additional gloomy features into the already dark picture of the dying Empire.[2]

[1] *Phrantzes*, 256 ; *Barbaro*, 33 ; *Leonardo*, 261.   [2] *Phrantzes*, 258.

3rd of May.—The Greeks placed four cannons on a tower which commanded the bay, and opened fire on the Turkish flotilla. The interchange of shots at this point was continued for several days without much effect.

In the city it was generally known that Venice and Naples, as well as the Pope, had promised to send help, and the southern horizon was watched day and night for the appearance of the allied fleet. As day after day passed and no sail appeared, the Emperor thought it desirable to send some one in search of the Latin fleet, and eventually to hasten its arrival at Constantinople; and in the night of this 3rd of May a small brigantine left the harbour and sailed out into the Marmara Sea. She carried the Turkish flag, and her crew were dressed *à la Turque*. This is stated in Barbaro's *Journal*,[1] while the *Slavonic Chronicler* says that on this day "*the Emperor sent men into the Morea, the islands, and to the countries of the Franks, to ask for help.*"[2]

The same day the Emperor presided at a great council; at this not only the military commanders, but also the dignitaries of the State and the Church assisted. The commandants of positions unanimously reported that movements observed in the Turkish camp indicated preparations for a general assault.

---

[1] *Barbaro*, 35.
[2] *Slavonic Chronicler*, 14.

Considering the condition of the walls, and the weariness of the diminishing defensive forces, none could speak confidently about the prospects of again repulsing the Turks. The senators and the prelates, with the Patriarch at their head, advised the Emperor to leave the city and retreat to a more secure place. Some of them expressed their conviction that the people of the provinces, so soon as they heard that the Emperor was alive and safe outside the besieged capital, would send to him numbers of volunteers, and that these, together with the armies of the Princes Demetrius and Thomas, and with the Albanians, whom Scanderbeg would not fail to bring, might make a diversion sufficiently important to alarm the Sultan, and force him to withdraw from the city.

Giustiniani himself energetically supported these representations, and placed all his ships at the Emperor's disposal.

"*The Emperor,*" continues our chronicler, "*listened to all this quietly and patiently. At last, after having been for some time in deep thought, he began to speak: 'I thank all for the advice which you have given me. I know that my going out of the city might be of some benefit to me, inasmuch as all that you foresee might really happen. But it is impossible for me to go away! How could I leave the churches of our Lord, and His servants the clergy, and the throne, and my people in such a plight? What would the world say about me?*

I pray you, my friends, in future do not say to me anything else but, " Nay, sire, do not leave us !" Never, never will I leave you ! I am resolved to die here with you !' And saying this, the Emperor turned his head aside, because tears filled his eyes; and with him wept the Patriarch and all who were there !" [1]

These were words of a noble and generous heart, words worthy of an Emperor. Constantine Dragasses, even on that occasion, did honour to the throne he occupied and to the nation of whom he was the chief.

4th of May.—The cannonade and occasional firing from the rifles went on as usual. Nothing specially noteworthy happened during the day.

But during the night from the 4th to the 5th of May, another attempt was made to destroy the Turkish ships in the bay. This time the attack was undertaken by a captain of one of Giustiniani's ships. The Turks, however, kept a sharp look-out, and when the Genoese galley quietly approached she was received with a full broadside and sunk at once.

5th of May.—The city was full of rumours of the last night's misfortune. The report was spread that Giustiniani himself was on the unlucky galley and had escaped with great difficulty. And again it was generally asserted that the Turks had received forewarning from a traitor.[2]

---

[1] *Slavonic Chronicler,* 116.   [2] *Ducas,* 277.

A new feature in the general excitement was produced by the sudden opening of fire from Zagan-Pasha's battery against the Christian ships posted along the harbour chain. For that purpose Zagan had obtained some heavier guns than those which he had at first.

A heavy ball struck a Genoese merchant ship, laden with silk and other costly freight, valued at 12,000 ducats. The ship foundered quickly after it was struck. The Christian fleet was obliged to leave its position and to move outside the chain, out of the reach of Zagan's cannons.[1]

The Genoese of Galata sent a formal protest to the Sultan against the damage done to those who were perfectly neutral. The Grand-Vizier returned elaborate excuses, and promised that after the conquest of the city the damage should be fully compensated.[2]

6th of May.—The Turks brought more cannon opposite the gate of St Roman. All the day long they maintained a steady fire. Towards evening a wide breach had been opened near that gate. To prevent the defenders filling the gap the Turks continued firing at that point all night. Giustiniani, however, did not attempt to repair the breach, but somewhat further inside raised barricades and a tower.[3]

7th of May.—The Turks continued to widen the

[1] *Barbaro* 36. [2] *Ducas*, 279. [3] *Slavonic Chronicler*, 118.

breach with concentrated fire from their great battery. Towards the evening the firing ceased.

About eleven o'clock at night great numbers of Turks rushed across the glacis, descended into the ditch, and hurried towards the breach. Barbaro says that about 30,000 Turks were ordered to this assault.

The Slavonic chronicler gives some interesting details of the fight. According to him, the Greeks and the Latins bravely went into the breach to meet the assailants, and fought with great fury. Giustiniani personally commanded, and was nearly killed by a Janissary of gigantic size. Reinforcements were brought to the Turks by a famous Turkish hero, Omer, a Sandjak-Bey from Romania. At the same moment Giustiniani was also reinforced by a company of Greeks under a very popular commander, Stratyg (Colonel) Rangabe, and by a gallant onslaught drove the Turks from the breach into the moat. Rangabe, cheering his men, led the way, and, clearing his path by the sword, he suddenly found himself face to face with the brave and famous Omer-Bey. "*Rangabe,*" continues our chronicler, "*immediately attacked him, and bracing one of his legs against a stone he lifted his sword with both hands and cut Omer-Bey in two. The Turks, enraged by the loss of such a hero, surrounded and cut to pieces Rangabe. Then the Greeks turned and retreated inside the walls. There were terror and general grief over the loss of Rangabe, the brave and gallant knight, whom the Emperor loved greatly."*

On the 8th, 9th, 10th and 11th of May nothing remarkable happened.

The Turkish cannonade continued as usual. This means, according to Tedardi, that besides a great number of smaller balls (weighing between 200 and 500 pounds), some 100 to 120 of heavier balls (weighing between 800 and 1200 pounds) were thrown against the walls and into the city.

In Constantinople itself the popular depression increased daily. Prayers were going on in the churches incessantly with much fear and many tears. Great crowds pressed constantly to kiss the holy picture of " Maria, Mother of God," which, according to the legend, had once already saved the city from its enemies, and might in mercy save it again. This "miraculous eikon" was exposed to the devotions and donations of pious people in the church of the Madonna Chodogetria near the Acropolis and St Sophia.

As it was evident that the fleet could not materially aid the defence, the Venetians began to disarm their ships. On the 9th of May, Gabrielo Trevisani left his two galleys, and with their crew, numbering some 400 men, went to strengthen the position of St Roman, where the losses in men were naturally heaviest.

12th of May.—The Turkish cannon battered a breach in the walls near the imperial palace of Hebdomon. Before the Greeks were able to begin the repairs in the evening, several thousands of Turks stormed that point. Barbaro has put down the storming force at 50,000 men; this is most likely an exaggeration.

According to the Slavonic Chronicle the Turkish onslaught was made with such vehemence that the Greeks were compelled to retire from the breach. The progress of the Turks was stopped by *Palæologus,* "*the Stratyg of Singurla,*" which some writers believe to mean "the commander of the cavalry," while others think it means "the assistant of the commander." Very probably it was Nicephoras Palæologus, who assisted his father-in-law, Cantacuzene, in the command of the reserves. The headquarters of the reserves were not far distant from the palace of Hebdomon, and therefore the help under Nicephoras Palæologus could arrive in good time.

But although Palæologus repulsed the Turks for the moment, he very soon became badly pressed himself, "because," according to our chronicler, "Mustapha-Pasha, Beyler Bey of Anadolia, sent fresh troops."

There arrived to the assistance of Palæologus, "Theodore, the commander of the Thousand, with Giustiniani." This commander, Theodore, in all probability was no other than Theodore of Karystos, who held the position of Charsias. The state of things at the Hebdomon seems to have been so critical that it was necessary to call not only the reserve, but also men from active service at other positions. But notwithstanding all this assistance, "*the Turks began to prevail against the Greeks*," as the Slavonic chronicler puts it.

On the same evening the Emperor was present with his suite at the vigil held in St Sophia. After the night service, which in the Greek Church takes two or three hours, the Emperor withdrew to one of the halls adjoining St Sophia, where he was met by the members of his Synklitos and some of the highest military commanders. There they improvised a military council. One of the generals, supported by the Logothet George Phrantzes, proposed that at a favourable moment a general sortie, under the command of the Emperor himself, should be undertaken. They pointed out two advantages of such a sortie: first the moral one, and next also the chance of capturing some provisions.

This proposal was opposed by Kyr Lucas Notaras and by the Prefect of the city, Nikola Goudeli. They thought it would be unwise to venture upon so hazardous an enterprise, but wiser to keep behind the walls, and be satisfied with defending themselves when attacked. "*We may well say,*" argued Kyr Lucas, "*that we have been fighting now already five months, and if it is God's will we can fight as many months longer; but without God's help, whatever we do, we shall all fall, and the city will be lost."* Kyr Lucas evidently considered that the war had commenced in December.

While they were thus discussing this important proposal a messenger arrived with the report that the Turks were on the walls behind the Hebdomon. The Emperor at once hurried off to the point of danger. In the streets he met crowds of people, and even armed men, fleeing from the walls. The Emperor stopped them, and ordered them back to their posts; but his bodyguards were obliged to use their swords and lances to force the panic-stricken soldiers to go back to the walls.

On his arrival at the Hebdomon the Emperor found the Turks had pressed through the breach and were fighting with the Greek and Latin volunteers in the adjoining streets! The Emperor's arrival with a few companies of soldiers gave fresh courage to the Christians already engaged, and with new and combined efforts they threw the Turks outside into the moat. "*If the Emperor had not arrived with fresh assistance, that same night would have seen our final destruction,*" says the Slavonic chronicler.[1]

To this fight probably belonged another incident which the same chronicler reports incidentally on

[1] *Slavonic Chronicler*, 12.

another occasion. The Emperor himself was so much excited by the desperate struggle, that he spurred his horse and galloped to the breach, evidently intending to ride through it into the ditch, where fighting hand to hand was still going on, "*but the nobles of the Imperial suite and his German guards stopped him and prevailed on him to ride back.*" [1]

The Turkish loss in this assault was currently reported the next day at about 10,000 men. More trustworthy is the statement that the Prefect of the city ordered all the bodies of the killed Turks to be thrown outside the fortifications, to be taken away by the commanders of the nearest Turkish positions.

14th of May.—The Turks were seen transporting some cannon from Zagan-Pasha's battery (the hill above Galata). It was believed they were going to strengthen the battery opposite the Kynegion. But they only stopped there some time for rest, and then carried the cannon to the position opposite the gate of St Roman.

This concentration of artillery was an additional indication that the principal attack would be directed against the position in Giustiniani's charge. Therefore a new company of some 400 well-armed men was organized, picked up from ships, and from other less exposed positions on the walls, and placed under Giustiniani's command.[2]

[1] *Slavonic Chronicler*, 17.   [2] *Barbaro*, 40.

15th of May.—The day passed away without any special incident.

16th of May.—Some Turkish galleys approached the Christian fleet, which seems to have regained its original position within the harbour chain. After the inefficient exchange of some shots the Turkish ships withdrew to their anchorage.

17th of May.—Some time before, the Greek headquarters had received information of the arrival of Saxon miners in the Turkish camp. These miners were from Novo Brdo (otherwise known as Novo-Monte or Neue-Berghe), a celebrated silver mine in Serbia, worked since the middle of the thirteenth century by a colony of Saxons. Their arrival was understood to mean energetic attempts to undermine the walls. And really on the night of the 17th of May, Johannes Grant succeeded in discovering and destroying a Turkish mine, in which a great number of workmen and soldiers were buried alive.

18th of May.—At the earliest dawn the watchmen at the Charsias Gate noticed a peculiar structure on the other side of the ditch.

A high wooden tower made of strong beams and boards, covered with buffalo hides, and placed on wheels, had been pushed within 10 or 12 yards of the ditch. It had two stories, the sides of the lower being enclosed by thick boards, and the space between them filled with earth. The upper floor, which could be reached by a number of ladders, was specially protected by buffalo hides. The tower had three openings, like wide windows, facing the city, and from these the archers and riflemen could easily shoot at the men on the walls. From the tower a covered way led to the first line of the Turkish camp.[1]

In general, this day of the 18th of May was full of misfortunes for the Greeks. The Turkish archers from the Buffalo Tower caused them great loss of men at the position of Charsias; and one of the towers at the gate of St Roman and part of the adjoining wall fell into the moat under the reinforced fire of the great battery.

In the bay the Turks had completed their barrel-bridge leading towards the north-eastern gate of the Kynegion.[2] It was 250 yards long, and $2\frac{1}{2}$ yards wide. It had evidently been the intention of the Turkish commander-in-chief to attempt to storm at the same time two distant points, the gate of St Roman and the gate of Kynegion, hoping thus to divide the forces of the besieged.

On the night of the 18th of May the Emperor Constantine and Giustiniani made almost superhuman efforts. They succeeded in filling in the breach at St Roman's Gate, and raised a new tower to defend that position; they organized a company of gallant

[1] *Phrantzes*, 244; *Barbaro*, 42.
[2] *Barbaro*, 143; *Ducas*, 279; *Chalcochondylas*, 450; *Phrantzes*, 252.

volunteers, who climbed the counterscarp, and threw Greek fire into the Buffalo Tower, burning it to ashes. The boldest men among the Turks, even Sultan Mohammed himself, could not suppress their astonishment, and openly expressed their admiration of the skill and energy of the defenders. The Sultan is reported to have said concerning the new tower: "*If yesterday all the thirty-seven thousand prophets had told me that such a feat was possible, I would not have believed it!*"[1]

On the 19th and 20th of May nothing happened worthy of special attention.

21st of May.—The trumpets sounded very early on board the ships of the Turkish fleet, which left its anchorage before the Diplokynion, and sailed slowly towards the entrance of the Golden Horn. The signal of alarm was given in the city, the soldiers rushed to the walls, and the people with fear and trembling filled the streets. But about seven o'clock the Turks steered suddenly back to their usual position.

In the afternoon of the same day another Turkish mine approaching the walls of Kalligaria was detected and destroyed.

The Turkish cannon made a fresh breach in one place, and brought down part of a tower. Barbaro heard of this, but did not catch the name of the place. He only mentions the fact, and added that

[1] *Barbaro*, 44.

the succeeding night the Greeks repaired the damage.[1]

22nd of May.—Grant's pioneers detected two Turkish mines in Kalligaria and destroyed them. In one they had to engage in a hand-to-hand struggle with the Turkish workmen and soldiers, killing every one of them.

Though the nature of the soil, which had prevented the making of a ditch in front of Kalligaria, was not well adapted for the laying of mines, yet the pioneers on both sides developed no little skill and boldness in this particular form of warfare. How active they were may be seen from Totardi's report. He says: "Zagan-Pasha, with his men accustomed to gold and silver mines, had undermined the fortifications on 14 different points, having commenced digging at great distance from the walls. The Christians, on their side, by listening, discovered the positions of the Turkish mines, and made counter-mines. By smoke, sometimes by bad odours, they suffocated the Turks in their subterranean galleries. In some places they drowned them by admitting water, and at other times they fought them hand to hand."[2]

The Slavonic chronicler states the Greeks often went during the nights into the ditch, and through the brickwork of the counterscarp undermined the glacis. He describes graphically the explosion of one of these

[1] *Phrantzes*, 247; *Barbaro*, 45.   [2] *Informacion*, p. 25.

mines. "It was," he says, "as if the lightning had struck the place, for the earth shook and with a great crash a greenish whirlwind carried the Turks into the air. Fragments of men and timber fell into the city and into the camp. The besieged ran away from the walls and the besiegers fled back from the ditch."[1]

[1] *Slavonic Chronicler*, 12.

CHAPTER VII.

THE LAST DAYS.

ON the 23rd day of May a few Turkish horsemen approached the gate of St Roman with sounding trumpets and waving flags, giving the guard on the tower to understand that they had a communication to make. A special envoy of the Sultan desired to deliver a message to the Emperor personally. After some time an answer was given from the walls that the envoy might enter the city.

This envoy, Ismail Hamza, the Lord of Sinope and Kostamboly, son of the late Isphendiar-Khan, was related by marriage to the Padishah himself. The Isphendiar-Khans were for some time independent princes who had energetically resisted absorption into the great Ottoman Empire; but at length they were obliged to acknowledge the suzerainty of the Sultan, and reconciled themselves to what seemed inevitable. The Isphendiar-Khans had been for generations on friendly terms with the Greek Emperors, and Ismail Hamza was received by the Emperor as an old friend.

Hamza delivered and explained the Sultan's

message. As the situation of the city was unmistakably hopeless, why should the Emperor prolong the miseries of war, and expose his people to the terrible consequences of the storming of the place? The Sultan entertained sincere and deep respect for the Emperor, and would permit him to withdraw unmolested, together with his Court, noblemen, and treasures, wherever he desired to go. Nay, more than this, the Sultan again offered to the Emperor the suzerainty of the Peloponnesus. The inhabitants of Constantinople would also be allowed to depart with their portable property, if they chose to go; and to all who preferred to remain, the Sultan guaranteed security of persons and possessions. The Emperor must consider this as the Sultan's last summons to him to surrender. If rejected, the horrors of a sack could not be spared to the city.

Then Hamza, speaking less as the Sultan's envoy than as the Emperor's friend, sought to induce Constantine to accept the apparent decrees of destiny. The walls on the land side were broken through in several places, four towers were quite destroyed, the small garrison could not be otherwise than exhausted, and there was no prospect of a speedy arrival of help from without.

These arguments were unfortunately all undeniable facts. The actual condition of the city was even more deplorable. Provisions were becoming every day scarcer; the people had sunk into a state of stolid despair; they considered the Emperor and his Government responsible for the sufferings they had already undergone, and for the still greater misfortunes which threatened them. It was evident that the Virgin Mary could not be induced either by prayers or by tears to appear again on the walls and disperse the enemy. "But," asked some orthodox Greeks, "was it any wonder that, after the desecration of St Sophia and abominations of the 12th of December, their supplications to Heaven were unheeded?" Others said: "No doubt our fathers and forefathers have sinned and we have sinned ourselves, and it is right in God's providence that we should be punished. All these misfortunes are evidently $K\tau\acute{\eta}\mu a\ \tau o\hat{v}\ \theta\epsilon o\hat{v}$, 'God's punishment.' Why seek to escape that punishment? Is it right to continue to fight, and to oppose God's manifest will?"

Not only the battered walls, but still more the broken spirit of the mass of the people, and the unfulfilled promises of foreign assistance, would have given Constantine a reasonable justification for honourable surrender.

But Constantine had a more lofty conception of his own dignity and duty. According to Ducas, he returned by Hamza the following answer to the Sultan:—

"I should praise God if thou wouldst live in peace with us, as thy forefathers did; they treated my predecessors with filial respect, and this city with the greatest consideration. Whoever of them was persecuted by misfortune and came to us was safe; but whoever raised a hand against our city never prospered. Retain as thy rightful possession the territories which thou hast unjustly taken from us, and settle the amount of the tribute, which we will do our utmost to pay every year, and then go in peace. Remember, that grasping the possessions of others, thou mayest thyself become the prey of others! To surrender the city is neither in my power nor in the power of any one here. We are all prepared to die, and shall do so without regret!" [1]

Early on the morning of the 24th of May a small ship approached the chain closing the harbour. The crew were apparently Turks, but after the exchange of signals with the Venetian ships keeping guard, the chain was lowered, and the vessel was admitted within the harbour.

It proved to be the ship which some twenty days previously had been despatched in search of the allied fleet. Its commander had called at many islands of the Archipelago, everywhere making inquiries, and leaving word for the allies to hasten to Constantinople. But he nowhere fell in with them. For a time he and his men were undecided how to act, as it was almost hopeless to return. But in the end they

[1] *Ducas*, 266.

felt it their duty to go back, and not to leave their good Emperor to prolonged anxiety and uncertainty. And so they returned with their most discouraging report, and arrived only in time to die. Unfortunately, the name of that gallant captain has not been preserved![1]

On this day Johannes Grant discovered and destroyed a very dangerous mine, which had been extended about ten yards beneath the wall of Kalligaria.[2]

The Turkish cannonade continued all day without intermission. After sunset the entire Turkish camp was illuminated, and at the same time numerous lanterns were hoisted on the masts of the vessels at Diplokynion. Great rejoicings were made both on board the ships and in camp. Wild Turkish music, with a predominance of big drums, cymbals, and shrill nacaires, resounded the whole distance from the Golden Horn to the Sea of Marmara.

The Emperor Constantine rode out as usual to visit the posts of his army. At several points he dismounted and went on the walls to observe that great fiery crescent which seemed to encircle the Imperial City. He listened to the monotonous beating of the drums, and to the wild tumult that prevailed in the Turkish camp. Constantine and the few gallant men who shared with him the burden and

---

[1] *Barbaro*, 46.   [2] *Barbaro*, 47.

responsibility of the defence recognized in that spectacle the precursor of a general assault. We are told that while gazing on the illuminated and noisy camp of the enemy, the Emperor remained silent, wrapped in thought, while tears ran down his cheeks.[1] He was not, he had no need to be, ashamed of his tears, as he was resolved bravely to do his duty to the last.

The great mass of the populace knew nothing of the rejoicings and of the numerous bonfires in the Turkish camp. Some of the citizens, while returning from the vigils in the churches, noticed the sudden appearance of the red light at the base of the great cupola of St Sophia. The light seemed to creep slowly up and round the cupola, until it reached the gilt cross above it. There it lingered for a few moments, and then the ruddy glare grew pale and paler, trembled for a few moments above the magnificent edifice, and then faded away. It was as though the sun, lingering awhile in the west, had looked back from behind the dark curtains of the night, to glance with a last loving ray on the finest temple in the Christian world, and to greet with a glow of reverence the cross so soon to be displaced by the crescent.

All this was merely a reflection from great bonfires in the Turkish camp, which the simple and superstitious people in the streets of Constantinople could not

[1] *Slavonic Chronicler*, p. 19.

see. To them it appeared a distinct sign from Heaven, full of meaning. Two eye-witnesses, Nicolo Barbaro and the writer of the *Slavonic Chronicle*, report that the citizens who saw the reflected light on the cupola were filled with fearful forebodings. Barbaro describes the whole scene as resembling an eclipse of the moon, reminding the people of an old prophecy "that the city would fall in the days when the moon should give a sign."[1]

According to the *Slavonic Chronicle*, the monks interpreted "the fearful sign" to the people in this way: "The holy light which dwelt in the church of St Sophia, and the angel whom God had in the time of the Emperor Justinian appointed to watch over this holy church and over the city, had that night departed to heaven in the pervading brightness so many people had seen. It was a sign that God meant to deliver the city into the hands of its enemies."[2]

The same night imperial messengers hurried through the streets, summoning all the state dignitaries and commanding officers to meet the Emperor early next morning.

25th of May.—The Council met very early, under the presidency of the Emperor. Such of its members as did not show signs of the fatigue of a night spent on the walls, bore the stamp of despair on their countenances. Never before, amidst the unrivalled

[1] *Barbaro,* 46.   [2] *Slavonic Chronicler,* 123.

beauties of the Golden Horn, and under the soft and balmy splendour of a May morning on the Bosphorus, had a body of patriots assembled under more mournful and desperate circumstances. With all their love for their country, they felt with intense bitterness that the old Byzantine Empire, hallowed by so many glories and grand traditions, was now dying on their trembling arms and broken hearts.

The Council had that morning to deliberate on the measures requisite in view of the expected assault.

The Emperor Constantine, simple, kind, brave and straightforward, had gained the sympathy and admiration of all who had witnessed his wonderful patience, forbearance, and untiring devotion to the public interests. All present at that last Council were animated by the deepest personal regard for the unhappy sovereign.

Some of the statesmen again brought before the Council the proposal that the interests of the Empire required the Emperor and his Court to leave the city immediately, inasmuch as so long as the Emperor lived there was hope that the capital, if lost now, might one day be regained.

The Prelate, who was at the head of the clergy, the Patriarch Gregory having apparently in the meantime resigned his office, supported with great decision that proposition. He said: "The servants of the altar saw unmistakable signs that it was God's will the city should now fall; but God's providence was unsearchable, and it might please Him to remember His people in mercy. If the Imperial City could not be saved, let the Emperor be saved! The Emperor should live, because in his person are centred the hopes of his people. We must all bow to the decree of the Almighty, whose mercy might return to our people as it had returned to Israel in olden times!"

The Prelate's words deeply moved all present. The *Slavonic Chronicler* says that the Emperor, on hearing that the Church also believed the fall of the city unavoidable, was so overpowered that he fainted, "*and it was necessary to use perfumed waters to revive him.*" Sleepless nights, constant work, crushing anxieties, and in addition the severe fasts with which he, as a true Greek, had doubtless supported his supplications to Heaven, had told upon his frame. However, he was again himself in a few moments. Then the Prelates pressed him to leave the city without delay, and the whole Council implored him to comply with this advice. After all who wished to speak had spoken, the Emperor addressed them in a quiet but resolute tone :—

"My friends, if it is God's will that our city shall fall, can we escape His wrath? How many emperors, great and glorious, before me have had to suffer and to die for their country! Shall I be the one to flee from it? No, I will stay and die here with you!"[1]

This determination of the Emperor to remain faithful to what he believed his duty rendered further discussion of his departure superfluous. But it was then probably decided to send away the Princess Helene, the widow of the Despot Demetrius, with the ladies of her Court. When, after the taking of the city, the Sultan inquired what had become of the imperial ladies, he was told that one of Giustiniani's ships had carried them away.[2]

The Council passed on to the discussion of other questions. It was resolved that all men, without distinction, must assist in repairing breaches in the walls. This resolution was adopted after Giustiniani had bitterly complained that the Greeks had refused to aid in repairing the walls at St Roman's, declaring it to be the duty of the Latin warriors whom he commanded.

After this, Giustiniani declared it to be imperative that his position should be strengthened by additional artillery, and he suggested that some guns might be brought from the positions along the Golden Horn, which were not much exposed to danger. Kyr Lucas Notaras, the commander-in-chief of those positions, absolutely refused to give any of his cannon. It came

---

[1] *Slavonic Chronicler*, 127. *Phrantzes* incidentally confirms the Slavonic report, saying, "the Emperor could have left the place, but he would not."—Lib. iv. c. 2, p. 327.

[2] *Ibid.*

to sharp words between these two, and the matters were drifting to a discreditable scene, when the Emperor, with his usual forbearance and kindness, interposed. "My friends," said he, "this is not the time for quarrels; rather let us bear with each other, and pray God to save us from the mouth of the Turkish serpent!"[1]

But the haughty remarks of Kyr Lucas had piqued the ambition of the brave and energetic Giustiniani. He returned to his post, and by the help of some men, amongst whom the Archbishop of Chios specially mentions a certain Ivan of Dalmatia, he succeeded that day and the next night in repairing his walls so well that both friends and enemies were astonished. The Sultan is reported to have exclaimed: "Why have I not such men!"[2]

Late in the evening of this day a new Turkish mine was detected and destroyed in Kalligaria.

26th of May.—The enemies fired as usual. In the city preparations to meet the expected attack were continued with feverish zeal.

The same day a diplomatic reception took place in the spacious tent of the Sultan. The embassy from the new King of Hungary, Vladislaus, was received in solemn audience. According to Turkish etiquette, the

---

[1] *Phrantzes*, 262; *Ducas*, 181; *Chalcochondylas*, 452; *Barbaro*, 48.

[2] The Archbishop Leonardo, relating this, adds that attempts were made on the part of the Sultan to bribe Giustiniani (p. 262).

ambassador was not permitted to speak directly to the Sultan about the object of his mission, but after the audience he had an interview with the Grand-Vizier in the presence of two Pashas of the highest rank. The ambassador gave official notification of King Vladislaus' accession to the throne, and expressed the friendly desire of the young King that the Sultan would withdraw his army from before Constantinople, as otherwise Hungary could not help joining the league formed by the Pope against the Turks. If the Grand-Vizier was not earlier acquainted with the fact of the Venetian squadron being on its way to Constantinople, he heard it now from the Hungarian ambassador.

Immediately after this interview very alarming reports began to spread through the Turkish camp. It was rumoured that the Hungarian ambassador brought a declaration of war, and that "*the redoubtable white knight Voyvode Yanko*" (as the Turks called John Hunyadi) had already crossed the Danube with a large army, and was marching on Adrianople, while a powerful "Latin fleet" was not far from the Dardanelles. Phrantzes says that Chalil's own agents tried to incite the alarmed soldiers to speak against the inexperienced young Sultan, whose recklessness would bring their fine but now almost exhausted army between three fires![1]

That evening, again, great illuminations were to be

[1] *Phrantzes*, 264.

seen in the Turkish camp. But though the big drums beat louder, and the "Zurnes" shrieked more wildly than ever, the topics around the numerous bonfires were not of a cheering nature. The Sultan himself, according to Phrantzes, had a sleepless night. The message brought by the Hungarian ambassador, the reports about the approaching fleet, the dissatisfaction amongst his soldiers, combined to keep him awake. And the uncertainty as to the decisions of the great war council he had convened for the next morning, was in itself enough to drive away slumber from a less ambitious man than Sultan Mohammed.

27th of May.—The great Council met in the Padishah's own tent. Everyone felt that matters had reached a most critical point.

Chalil-Pasha laid before the Sultan and the Council his own view of the situation. Some pity could hardly be refused to that old man in his peculiar position. He knew well that he was surrounded by envious and suspicious persons, who were watching keenly for the least false step of the Vizier, whom they already liked to call "Giaour-Yoldash." But after all, Chalil was no traitor. He believed sincerely, and had courage to say, that the risks were greater than the chances of success. As an old and faithful servant of the Ottoman throne, he gave frank expression to his fears, without caring for the possible consequences to himself.

Chalil stated that, according to the reports received, all Europe was rising to the assistance of Constantinople. If the united Franks once reached that city, they would not be satisfied with only driving away the Turks from its walls, they might, and most probably would, undertake to drive them altogether out of Europe. The persistent attempt to take Constantinople only brought increasing risks of losing all the European provinces their ancestors had conquered. "I have often told your Majesty," said the Grand-Vizier in conclusion, "the probable results of this undertaking. I have pointed out to you the risks you ran; but you did not heed my counsel. Now, for the last time, I am bold enough to implore you: let us raise the siege lest worse evils befall us!"[1]

Chalil spoke with great humility, but with decision. His bowed frame, his white beard, his careworn expression and earnest dark eye, presented the very picture of an anxious, wise statesman, desirous to serve his country well. The Sultan, at that moment at least, did not suspect the loyalty of his old adviser, and was visibly impressed by his earnestness.

Zagan, the chief of the Turkish Chauvinists, felt the great importance of the moment. To withdraw from Constantinople meant banishment from Court, if not the silken cord for him and his friends, who had encouraged the Sultan to undertake the siege. Inde-

[1] *Phrantzes*, 266.

pendently of these personal considerations, Zagan was a fiery Turkish patriot, a man of strong and resolute will, well informed about the true state of affairs not only in the Balkan Peninsula, but throughout Europe.

"With regard to the Grand-Vizier's assertions," said Zagan, "that the allied Franks are coming to the assistance of Constantinople, I do not believe it for a moment. Nor is it likely that the Latin fleet will speedily appear. Thou, O Padishah, knowest well the great dissensions that are raging in Italy especially, and in all Frankistan generally. In consequence of these dissensions the Giaours are incapable of united action against us. The Christian potentates never will unite together. When after protracted efforts they conclude something like a peace amongst themselves, it never lasts long. Even when they are bound by treaties of alliance, they are not prevented seizing territories from each other. They always stand in fear of each other, and are busily occupied in intriguing against each other. No doubt they think much, speak much, and explain much, but after all they do very little. When they decide to do anything, they waste much time before they begin to act. Suppose they have even commenced something, they cannot progress very far with it because they are sure to disagree amongst themselves how to proceed. And at present this is likely to be the case more than ever, because there are new causes for dissensions among them. Therefore there is no reason why we should fear them. Let us even, for the sake of argument, admit that the Latin fleet may arrive in Constantinople. What is that to us when their whole force is not equal to half, no, not to one-fourth of ours? There is at present no danger unless God sends one. Therefore, O Padishah, do not lose hope, but give us the order at once to storm the city!"

Zagan was a soldier, speaking in the presence of a Sultan who was completely in sympathy with the speaker by age, temper, and ambition.

In both speeches there was much that was wise and true. The Sultan thought he could not do better than to combine both views by a sort of compromise. At his suggestion the Council decided to try a general assault in the early morning of the 29th of May; if the assault succeeded, well and good; if it did not, the siege should be raised at once.

According to Phrantzes, a trusty messenger came from the Turkish camp into the city on the following night, and brought a detailed report to the Emperor of everything that had been spoken and decided in the council in the Sultan's tent. At the same time, the Emperor was advised not to lose courage, but to hope for the best, to place picked troops on the land walls, to be watchful, and to fight resolutely.[1]

[1] *Phrantzes*, 269.

This Sunday evening (27th of May) the Turkish camp and fleet were again illuminated. The Tellals were running in all directions, shouting the Padishah's orders: "The faithful might enjoy themselves as much as they liked this night; to-morrow they must fast and pray, so that each one who was predestined to enter Paradise should be ready to be gathered to the martyrs for the faith next Tuesday morning!"

The knowledge that the storming of the city would begin the day after the morrow caused fresh excitement in the camp. All the night the Dervishes and Ulemas went from one fire to another, and from group to group of soldiers, rousing their enthusiasm by their fantastic gestures and more fantastic speeches. Zagan-Pasha himself, by command of the Sultan, went in disguise amongst the tents, listening to the conversation of the soldiers, and was able to lay before the Sultan, in the early morning of the 28th of May, a satisfactory report of the spirit pervading the army.[1]

Monday, 28th of May.—Early in the morning the trumpets resounded through the Turkish camp, giving a signal that all the troops should take the positions assigned to them, and that no soldier should leave his company.

The squadron in the Golden Horn deployed in a line, facing the walls along the bay. The whole fleet

---

[1] *Phrantzes, loc. cit.*

at Diplokynion left its moorings, and took up a position in the form of a crescent, stretching from a point opposite the harbour to the gate of Theodosius (Vlanga-Bostan-Kapoussi).

The Turkish batteries fired as usual up to about four o'clock in the afternoon, when their firing abruptly ceased.

A short time after the cessation of the cannonade great cheering was heard from the Turkish camp. The Sultan, accompanied by a brilliant suite, visited each troop in its position. Here and there he stopped to address a few words to the soldiers. Then the following manifest was made to the army:—

"During the assault many soldiers, according to the immutable law, must fall. But bear in mind that it is written: He who falls fighting for the faith will enter directly into Paradise. They who survive after the conquest of the city will for life receive double pay. If the city is taken, you will have licence to pillage it for three days. All its wealth, its silver, gold, silk, cloth, and women, will be yours; only the buildings and the walls will be reserved for the Sultan."

The excitement among the Turks increased greatly after this "order of the day" had been read. And as the evening rays gilded for the last time the cross of St Sophia, the clamour of the thousands of warriors and camp-followers echoing from the Golden Horn to the

Sea of Marmara bore aloft the cry, "*La illah il-Allah, Mohammed ressoul-Allah!*"—"There is only one God, and Mohammed is his prophet!"

Alas, did any of those who watched the Turkish tents from the walls of Constantinople, in the light of that setting sun, feel that this was the last evening of Christian Constantinople?

Slowly the fires were lit in the Turkish camp. They burnt some time, and towards midnight were extinguished, and then all was quiet.

CHAPTER VIII.

The Last Night.

During the preceding two days (26th and 27th of May) the repairs of the walls had been pushed on with even increased activity. The Emperor personally superintended and urged on the work, reminding the men that not one hour must be lost.

On Monday morning—his last morning—the Emperor was again obliged to interpose his patient and lenient authority between the Latins and the Greeks. The Venetian Baylo had constructed some movable wooden shelters for his archers. He asked a number of Greeks to carry these wooden fences to the Venetian posts, but the Greeks refused, unless paid in advance. The Venetians felt indignant, especially as they believed the refusal came from the Greeks' hatred of Latins. But in this case the want of food, more than any other motive, had prompted the Greek answer. The Emperor stopped the quarrel, and found means to satisfy the angry Venetians.

The greater part of the morning the Emperor was occupied in the marshalling of his troops on the walls.

Ducas says that there were now altogether scarcely 4000 fighting men in the city.[1]

A procession started early from St Sophia, to the solemn pealing of the church bells, visiting the more celebrated churches on its way to the city walls. The priests, wearing their ancient and stiff vestments of gold brocade, carried many miraculous eikons, bones of the saints, golden and jewelled crosses containing "particles of the Holy Tree," and many other relics, in the possession of which the Greek Churches were so rich. Multitudes of people, old and young—men, women, and children—followed, most of them barefooted, weeping, sighing, and beating their breasts with their fists, men joining in the chanting of the clergy and in the singing of the psalms.

At every important position the entire procession stopped for a short time. The priests read special prayers that God would strengthen the walls of the city, and grant victory to His faithful people. The bishops then raised their croziers and blessed the soldiers, sprinkling them with holy water from bunches of dried basylicum. Some present, doubtless, thought with deep sadness that this was perhaps the last blessing which the Christian Church might give to the Christian soldiers on the walls of Constantinople.

In the afternoon, before the hour for Vespers, the

[1] *Ducas*, 283. Phrantzes exaggerates when he says that the proportion of the defenders to the assailants was as 1:500.

Emperor assembled around him (it is not said where, but most likely at the headquarters) the commanders of the troops and the chief citizens. He addressed them in touching words, asking all and every one not to spare themselves, and not to regret the shedding of their blood in defence of the glorious old city. Turning to the Venetians, who stood on his right hand, he reminded them that Constantinople had always welcomed them as sons. "I pray you now," continued the Emperor, "show us in this difficult hour that you are indeed our companions, our faithful allies, and our brethren!"

Then he turned towards the Genoese, spoke of their glorious past, and asked them to prove once more on this momentous occasion their world-renowned courage. The Emperor concluded with these few words addressed to all present: "Let us work together, my companions and my brethren, to gain for ourselves liberty, glory, and eternal memory! Into your hands I commit now my sceptre. Here it is! Save it! Crowns await you in heaven, and on earth your names will be remembered honourably until the end of time!"[1]

"Let us die for faith and Fatherland!" "Let us die for the Church of God and for thee, our Emperor!"

---

[1] The whole address is given by *Phrantzes*, pp. 271-278, who of course repeated only from memory what he had heard and seen on that occasion.

were the enthusiastic responses of those assembled around Constantine. All were deeply moved. Phrantzes, who was himself present, writes: "The defenders of the city embraced each other, and through tears kissed one another, asking and giving mutual pardon; no one thought more of wife, child, or property, but only of the glorious death which all were ready to meet for the sake of the Fatherland!"

The bells rang for Vespers.

The Emperor proceeded to St Sophia. The church was crowded. It would have been only natural for him to think that it was, perhaps, the last time he would stand beneath that magnificent cupola, under which so many orthodox Emperors had worshipped in good and evil days.

Constantine prayed with great fervour. He left his imperial chair, and approaching the screen separating the altar from the nave, he prostrated himself before the great eikons of Christ and of the Madonna, which were on the left and on the right side of the central entrance to the altar. Having passed some time in prayer, he approached every prelate present in the church, asked them to pardon him if he had ever offended any of them, embraced each of them, and then went to the altar and received the Holy Communion. As a Christian emperor, and as a Christian soldier, he was solemnly, and in the sight of his people, preparing to appear before his God.

When he turned to leave the church, the great congregation wept aloud. The vast church echoed with the loud sobs of men and with the wailings of women. And amidst such displays of sympathy from deeply moved human hearts, Constantine, himself greatly and visibly affected, walked slowly out of the church which his predecessors had raised as a grand monument of their glory and of their piety.

The Emperor next went to the imperial palace. There he had ordered all the dignitaries of state, all the courtiers and the servants of the Court, to await him. He said to them that no one could tell what the night would bring forth; he asked from each forgiveness for any harshness or injustice, and then he took a most touching leave of all. Phrantzes, who was in attendance upon the Emperor, says that it is impossible to describe the scene which ensued, nor the weeping and sobbing which shook the old palace. "It was a scene fit to melt a heart of stone!"[1]

Late in the evening Constantine left the palace, mounted his Arabian horse, and with his usual suite rode towards the walls to inspect for the last time the brave men who kept watch and awaited the end.

* * * * *

According to the *Slavonic Chronicler*, the evening of the 28th of May was sultry and gloomy. As night

[1] *Phrantzes, loc. cit.*

advanced, heavy and dark clouds slowly gathered above the city, like a pall dropped from heaven over this great mausoleum of marble and gold.

Sultan Mohammed, awake and restless, was struck with awe as he looked from his tent at the sky. He called one of his most learned Ulemas, well read in the mysteries of the heavens, and asked if the dense clouds hanging heavily over the city foreboded anything? "*Yes*," answered the Ulema; "*it is a great sign; it forebodes the fall of Stamboul!*"

"And then," says our informant, "from the clouds came not rain, but large drops of water, each drop almost as big as a bull's eye!"[1] Afterwards, some of the deeply impressed survivors of the catastrophe related, that a shower of blood sprinkled the city shortly before the desperate death-struggle began.[2]

Towards midnight, all the fires in the Turkish camp were extinguished.

It seemed as if the Byzantine Bosphorus passed its last midnight in deep sleep. It looked as if this sultry night of May could not tear itself from the beautiful city of the Christian emperors. It seemed as if deaf and dumb midnight hesitated to lift up the dark, cloudy veil from the Turkish camp, lest the morning star might too early awake the day, which was to see for the first time the Moslem Stamboul.

In the city all appeared quiet. Only on the paved

[1] *Slavonic Chronicler*, 19.   [2] *Ibid.*

streets near the walls were to be heard from time to time the echoes of horses' hoofs. About an hour after midnight some horsemen halted by the position near Kalligaria Gate. Dismounting, they ascended the walls. It was the Emperor with some of his faithful suite. They strained their eyes in the darkness towards the Turkish camp. They could see nothing. But they heard distinctly rumbling sounds and voices subdued in tone. The Emperor inquired of the watchmen what these peculiar sounds meant, and was told that apparently the Turks were advancing all their first line, and that possibly the rattling arose from the placing of ladders in the moat. The Emperor peered anxiously into the darkness, listening silently. Who could say what he thought and what he felt at that moment! Then the cocks began their first crow.

The Emperor rode quietly back to the position of St Roman. He had found watchfulness, readiness, and determination on the whole line. The men whom he had just seen, and who are now seen only through the shadows of more than four centuries, were brave men.

The second crowing of the cocks sounded from yard to yard, from street to street, and throughout the Turkish camp.

Suddenly the firing of a cannon shook the air, and awoke spreading echoes far and wide. With its dying thunder mingled war-cries from 50,000 throats along the Turkish line, and thousands of warriors glided swiftly down into the ditch, and hurriedly planted 2000 ladders against the city walls. The Christian soldiers sprang to arms, and the supreme struggle began.

According to the established rule in Turkish warfare of that time, the storming columns were arranged in three lines. The first line was formed of the poorest troops in the camp, with the undisciplined and untrained followers of the Ziyamet and Timariot Beys. The hardy mercenaries, many of whom were soldiers by profession, made the second line. The third line consisted of the highly trained companies of the Janissaries and the Spahis.

After an arduous fight, that lasted nearly an hour, the defenders of the walls successfully repulsed the first assault. Broad streams of Greek fire were poured from the walls on the dense crowds of the assailants, with more deadly effect than the showers of stones, arrows, and rifle bullets. At last the Turks in the moat were panic-stricken, and climbing in terror back, fled across the glacis.

But the unfortunate fugitives were met by a line of "Chaoushes" who forced them with iron maces and with chain-whips (Courbatch) back into the moat. The few who escaped the ferocious Chaoushes were encountered by the drawn scimitars of the Janissaries, and having only to choose between two deaths, returned back to the assault.[1]

Meanwhile the second line had been ordered to move forward. They advanced quickly and in good order to the sounding of trumpets and the beating of drums.

It must have been terrible in the pale yet increasing light of morning to see the dense columns, which like fierce billows broke against the walls, receded, and then again with still wilder fury dashed themselves higher up the ladders. The uproar is described as simply terrific. All the bells were ringing in the city, all the drums were beating in the camp, cannon and rifles were fired constantly from the city and against the city, and thousands of excited and almost maddened men shouted fiercely as they fought and fell.

About three o'clock in the morning a cannon ball tore down a piece of the outside wall near St Roman's Gate, at a point where the Venetians were posted. Upon this breach the Turks immediately concentrated their attack.

The Venetians, with the aid of some Greeks, repulsed the first onslaught. The next moment another ball widened the breach. Then a fresh column of Janissaries rushed forward, passed through the outside wall, and filled all the space between that and the inner wall, and reckless of danger planted there their scaling ladders and ascended them.

[1] For these details see *Phrantzes*, 285 ; *Barbaro*, 52.

The brave men who had already for more than two hours gallantly defended the position of St Roman began to waver. The Emperor sent for reinforcements. Theophilus Palæologus and Demetrius Cantacuzene hurried up with their men, and again the Turkish wave had to recede.

The Emperor saw the Turks fall back, and cheered on his men, shouting loudly to them: "*Bear yourselves bravely for God's sake! I see the enemy retires in disorder! If God wills, ours shall be the victory!*"[1]

While he still spoke a ball from a rifle struck the hand of Giustiniani.[2]

The wound caused him excessive pain; he became pale, and having said a few words to two Genoese officers, requesting one of them to take the command, he turned to leave the place.[3]

The Emperor, who stood but a few steps from him, was shocked to see the brave Giustiniani leave his post. "Whither art thou going, brother?" he asked. "I go," answered the pallid Giustiniani, "to see my wound attended to, and then I will return!"

The Emperor stepped nearer to him, looked at his wound, said it was not a dangerous one, and implored him to remain.

---

[1] *Phrantzes*, 283.

[2] *Ducas*, 284. According to others, Giustiniani was wounded in the foot.   [3] *Turco-Græcia*, p. 29.

Giustiniani paused an instant, hesitated, looked gloomily before him, and with the expression of great physical suffering on his face went away without a word.[1]

Extreme fatigue and intense physical pain had in that supreme hour shaken the heroic spirit of the man who had done so much for the defence of Constantinople, and who is denied immortal renown only by this one moment of weakness.

A group of Turks noticed confusion among the Christians at that particular point. Hassan Ulubadli, a Janissary of gigantic stature, hastily called on his companions to follow him, and ran up a ladder. Some thirty Janissaries crowded close at his heels, shouting loudly the name of Allah. Under showers of stones and arrows, half of them fell back into the moat wounded or killed. But Hassan sprang on the wall with a few of his comrades, and slashed fiercely about him with his scimitar. A fresh shower of stones and arrows struck him down, another shower wellnigh smothered him, but he rose on one knee and fought on, until at length, covered with wounds, he sank down and died. A gallant soldier and a true *Mussulman* was this Hassan Ulubadli.

At many other points of the land wall the fight

---

[1] *Phrantzes*, 283; *Ducas*, 160; *Leonardo*, 98; *Chalcochondylas*, 269. The words ascribed by Phrantzes to Giustiniani seem to me psychologically impossible, while those quoted by Ducas are far more natural.

raged with fierce and desperate fury. Sometimes it seemed that all the efforts of the choicest troops of the Sultan could not prevail against the grand old walls and the steadfast courage of their defenders.

But suddenly a man, apparently terror-struck, rode in great haste towards the spot where the Emperor stood, and shouted from the distance that the Turks had entered the city, and would speedily assail the rear of the Emperor's position!

This is what had happened.

In the walls which defended the palace and suburb of Hebdomon there was an old gate, quite low and on a level with the bottom of the moat, called "Kerko-porta." One of the Byzantine emperors had ordered it to be closed long ago because, as the legend runs, someone had prophesied that through that gate the enemy would enter the city. During the present siege the Greek general staff, when considering the plan of a sortie against the Turkish positions, had found that it would be easy for a large body of troops to issue through this old gateway and come unawares upon the left wing of the Turks. In preparation for such an emergency, the gate was reopened, and a guard told out to keep watch there. The proposed sortie had been abandoned, and during the great anxieties of the last days the Kerko-porta was quite forgotten.

While the main force of the assault was being concentrated against the position of St Roman, a body of Turks, passing in the moat along the walls, came unexpectedly upon this old low-lying gate and found it open. They rushed in, killed the few guards, hurried on upon the wall, and hoisted a lance with the horse-tail on the nearest tower! Other Turks followed them, running and shouting exultingly, and soon thousands had pressed into the city through this fatal gate. Kyr Lucas Notaras vainly tried to stem this torrent; his brave Greeks were speedily overpowered, he was forced to retreat, and with a remnant of his men shut himself up in his own palace, which was like a fortified castle.

Some Turks at once took possession of the palace of Hebdomon, while others hurried through the streets towards the position at St Roman's Gate. Their path was red with blood and strewn with wounded and dying men.

CHAPTER IX.

THE LAST HOURS.

THE report that the Turks had entered the city spread like wildfire.

The soldiers and people were panic-stricken at the sudden appearance of the enemies in their midst. Many Italians at once left their posts, and ran towards the harbour, where numbers of them succeeded in reaching the ships.

Crowds of people hastened to the church of St Sophia, filled it quickly almost to suffocation, and then fastened all the doors. Other crowds ran to and fro through the streets, not knowing in their despair where to go or what to do.

In some of the more distant streets women were seen walking with burning tapers in their hands; they were hurrying to the matin mass in the church of St Theodosia, whose festival was on this day. Soon they became alarmed by the distant uproar, and stopped and listened, until terrified men and women rushed breathlessly by, crying in horror the Turks were in the city. Thousands of half-dressed women and children fled in wild terror through the streets, as though an earthquake had suddenly left them homeless and maddened with fright. The shrieks of terror and wails of despair of the unfortunate Christians were rising to the skies, mingled with the exulting cries of the victorious Turks.

At the news of what had happened the Emperor stood for a few moments as if thunderstruck. The flight of the Italians towards the harbour caused some one in the imperial suite to suggest that there was, perhaps, still time for the Emperor to reach the harbour safely.

Constantine answered simply : *"God forbid that I should live an Emperor without an Empire ! As my city falls, I will fall with it !"*

The wild cries of the Turks were distinctly heard approaching from the neighbouring streets.

Constantine turned towards his suite, and said: *"Whoever wishes to escape, let him save himself if he can ; and whoever is ready to face death, let him follow me !"*[1]

Theophilus Palæologus answered the Emperor's last words, exclaiming: *"I would rather die than live !"*

Constantine spurred his horse, and he rode forward, sword in hand, to meet the Turks appearing in the next street. About two hundred Greek and Italian nobles and other volunteers followed the Emperor closely. Don Francesco di Toledo rode on the

[1] *Spandugin Cantacuzin, Comentari*, p. 190-6.

Emperor's right hand, while Demetrius Cantacuzene was on his left.

A few moments later they were all engaged in a fierce fight with the advancing crowds of Turks.

Ivan the Dalmatian spurred his horse into the midst of a company of Turks, and, as Phrantzes writes, "*mowed them down as though they were grass.*" He fell soon covered with wounds, dying the death of a hero at the post of honour.

Theophilus Palæologus, who so nobly preferred death to life, fell from his horse mortally wounded. The splendid Spaniard, Don Francesco, fought bravely for some time longer.

In the excitement of the fight the Emperor was soon separated from his followers. His Arabian horse fell under him, covered with blood and wounds. The Emperor on foot fought desperately on. An Assab struck him in the face. The Emperor cut him down with his sword, but the next moment fell forward mortally wounded.[1] Not one of the Turkish soldiers on the spot knew at that moment who the brave man was who had died fighting so valiantly.

The struggle continued some time around the spot, until heaps of slain covered the ground sanctified for ever by the heroic death of the last Greek Emperor.

---

[1] This can be taken as the description current at the Sultan's court, and used by *Sa'ad-ud-din*. It was also the popular tradition among the Greeks,—*Chansons Populaires*, p. 74.

* * * * *

The Turks in the first moments of excitement mowed down all whom they met. But as the dawn of the day was approaching, they were able to discern that in the principal streets no more fighting men remained, but only a crowd of terrified men, who seemed unable to think or act, and of women, who, at the sight of the Turks and their bloody scimitars, shrieked and fainted. Then the Turks ceased killing, and began to capture the people for slaves, binding men, women, and children indiscriminately with ropes.

Many of the Janissaries did not care for the slaves to be captured in the streets, but hastened to St Sophia. Most of them believed in the old legends, which had been diligently spread through the camp, that there was accumulated in the catacombs of that church an enormous treasure of gold, silver, and precious stones.

Those who first arrived found all the doors fastened. They broke open the principal entrance. The splendid interior of the sacred building produced no impression on these men thirsting for blood and hungry for prey. They proceeded at once to pillage the church, which was blazing with gold and silver ornaments, and to divide among themselves the thousands of men and women who had hoped to find shelter in God's house, and who now, in sight of the holy eikons, became the slaves of the Turks. The men were roughly bound

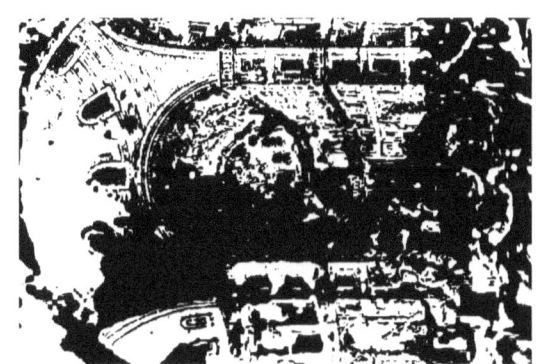

with ropes, in the presence of their wailing wives, mothers, and sisters. The poor women were fastened by their own girdles and long scarves. The saddest possible scenes of human agony were enacted under the grand cupola, amidst the resplendent marble columns, and on the beautiful mosaic pavement of the magnificent church. It was a picture which, with all its wealth in types of human beauty and ugliness, and all its richness of form and colour, still awaits the brush of a great artist. No other event in history can be compared with it, unless it be the fall of Jerusalem.

Before the arrival of the Turks, that part of the church where the altar stood was filled with the Greek clergy, some of them reading the Morning Service. When the Janissaries broke open the principal door, the priests had mysteriously disappeared. A legend was afterwards spread that at the approach of the Janissaries one of the church walls near the altar miraculously opened to admit the priest carrying the sacred chalice, and closed again after he had entered. According to the legend, the same priest will reappear, coming out from the same wall, to continue the interrupted service, on the day on which an orthodox Emperor reconquers Constantinople from the Turks.

The storming of the city had begun at about two o'clock in the morning of the 29th of May. About eight o'clock A.M. Constantinople was completely in the possession of the conquerors. In more outlying streets, and around some churches and strongly fortified houses, fighting still went on,[1] but this could not change the great fact that *early on Tuesday morning, the 29th of May, the Turks became masters of Constantinople.*

In the dawn of that fatal day the great and all-absorbing problem with most of the defenders of the city was, how they could save life and liberty. Those few morning hours must have been full of heart-stirring episodes. But only one or two of them have been recorded.

The Florentine Tedardi, and some other Italians, fought for full two hours after the Turks had entered the city, and, realizing at last the true situation, he tried to save himself, and passed through many perils before he reached the harbour. Once there, he threw himself into the waves, as so many other people did, and fortunately was soon picked up by a Venetian boat.

The captains of the ships in the harbour were untiring in their attempts to rescue the people. For this purpose they remained in the Golden Horn several hours after the capture of the city, sailing away only at noon.

Many fugitives crossed in small boats to Galata. Among these were the three brothers Brocciardi, who commanded at the position of Charsias.

---

[1] This is stated by *Phrantzes*, p. 288, as well as by the *Slavonic Chronicler*, and *Tedardi*.

Cardinal Isidore, with the aid of faithful servants, laid aside his purple robes, and put on the clothes of a common soldier. The body of a Latin volunteer was then dressed up in the robes of the Cardinal, and left lying in a street. The Turks came soon upon it, cut off the head of the supposed Cardinal, and carried it on a pike in triumph through the streets. Meanwhile, Isidore had fallen into the hands of other Turks; but he seemed so miserable and so useless as a slave that his Turkish master soon set him at liberty for a small sum of money.

The ill-fated pretender to the Turkish throne, Orchan-Effendi, let himself down on the beach from a tower of the Acropolis, disguised as a Greek monk. He roamed about there with some fugitive Greeks, in the expectation of being taken on board a Christian ship. A ship, indeed, came, but it was filled with Turks, who at once captured the fugitives. One wretched Greek bought his own freedom by betraying to the Turks who was the man in the monk's gown. Orchan-Effendi was instantly murdered, and his head sent to the Sultan.

The Turkish chronicles mention that a number of Greek monks—indeed as many as three hundred—the occupants of a monastery, seeing on that day on which side God was, and which was the true faith, declared themselves ready to accept Islam. It was certainly a day of terrible trial to many a heart once

P

full of faith, but now despairing amidst the ruins of an Empire.

*   *   *   *   *

Towards noon Mohammed entered the city by the gate of Poliandrium (Edirne-Kapoussi). He was accompanied by his Viziers, Pashas, and Ulemas, and escorted by his bodyguards, who were all men especially selected for their strength and manly beauty.

The Sultan rode straight to the Church of St Sophia. There he dismounted. At its threshold he stooped down, and collecting some earth he let it fall on his turbaned head, as an act of humiliation before God, who had given him the victory.[1]

Then he arose and entered the edifice, but in the doorway he stopped some moments and gazed in silence before him. The grand dimensions of the temple, its beauty and harmony, seemed to have a subduing effect on his spirit, even in that hour of triumph

Stepping forward, he saw a Turk breaking the mosaic floor with an axe. "*Wherefore dost thou that?*" asked the Sultan. "*For the Faith!*" replied the fanatic. Mohammed, in an impulse of anger, struck the man, saying angrily: "*You have got enough by pillaging the city and taking the citizens for slaves! The buildings are mine!*"

He advanced then further on towards the altar,

[1] *Slavonic Chronicler*, 21.

passing groups of his soldiers with their Christian slaves. Suddenly a door in the screen separating the altar from the nave was opened, and a number of priests came through it, and advanced to meet the Sultan. While still at some distance from him, they fell on their knees and cried: "Aman!" "Be merciful to us!"

Mohammed looked on them with pity. Our chronicler says: "He made a sign with his hand to the priests to rise, and said, 'Be not to-day afraid of my wrath, neither of death nor of pillage!' He then turned to his followers, and ordered them at once to send public criers to prohibit all further molestation of the people. And to the people in the church he said: 'Now, let every man go to his own home!'"[1]

This remarkable episode, described by the *Slavonic Chronicler*, is quite consistent with the character of Mohammed and with all other circumstances. It is most probable that the priests, at the approach of the Janissaries, retired to one of the secret passages in the walls, and there after some time decided to avail themselves of the Sultan's expected coming to the church, to implore his protection. Their disappearance for a time through a secret door in the cathedral walls would explain the origin of the legend we have already mentioned.

"The Sultan," continues the *Chronicler*, "waited for

[1] *Slavonic Chronicler*, 22.

some time until the people should quit the church: then unable to stay to the end, he himself departed."

From other sources we know that before he left the building, he ordered one of his Court-Ulemas to ascend the pulpit and deliver a prayer. He himself mounted on the marble table, which had been the Christian altar of St Sophia, and there made his first " Rika'at "—certain movements accompanying a Mussulman's prayer.

From that moment the St Sophia of the Christian Constantinople was transformed into the Aya-Sofia of the Mussulman Stamboul.

Coming out of the temple, Mohammed inquired of his suite, among whom were now several Greek dignitaries, whether any one knew what had become of the Emperor. No one had any certain information. Some thought that he had very likely fallen in the fight; others said more probably he had been carried away on the Italian ships which had sailed from the harbour. It is possible that even at that moment the version was current that the Emperor was amongst those who were squeezed to death when a panic-stricken crowd pressed through a gate.

As the Sultan proceeded along the street leading from St Sophia to the Acropolis, a Serbian soldier, carrying in his hand a man's head, met the imperial cavalcade. He lifted up the bloody trophy, shouting loudly to the Padishah, "*Glorious Lord (may happi-*

ness be always thine!), *this is the head of the Tzar Constantine!*"

The cavalcade halted. Kyr Lucas Notaras and some other Greek nobles were called to approach and look on the pale head.

At the first glance the Greeks burst into tears, and some of them sobbed aloud. It was the head of the Emperor.

The Serbian led some officers of the Sultan's suite to show them the body from which the head had been cut off. It was identified by the purple shoes on which the imperial double-headed eagles were embroidered. It was lying on the square now known by the name of Sandjakdar Yokushar.

The Sultan ordered that the Emperor's head should be exposed for some time on a column of porphyry which stood on the open space in front of the imperial palace. He wished the people of Constantinople to see that the last Greek Emperor was certainly dead.[1] But on the same day he gave permission to the Greek clergy to bury the Emperor's body with all the honours due to the imperial dignity. And to mark still more his personal regard for Constantine, he ordered that the oil to be burnt in a lamp at the grave of the last Greek Emperor should be defrayed from his own treasury.[2]

[1] *Phrantzes*, 291 ; *Ducas*, 300.

[2] To this day oil in the lamp at Constantine's grave is provided by the Ottoman Government.—*Mordtmann*.

The next day the Sultan installed himself in the palace in which the Byzantine Emperors had resided for centuries. Pillaging warriors had already stripped it completely of all that was portable. The great halls, which had glittered in gold and scarlet, were dismantled and bare.

The fate of the ancient Empire and the fate of its last Emperor stirred the heart of the young conqueror. His poetical instincts were aroused; he paused some time in deep thought, and then entered the large hall of the palace, reciting the verses of the Persian poet:

"*Now the spider draws the curtain in the Cæsars' palace hall,
And the owl proclaims the watch beneath Afrasiab's vaulted dome.*"

*   *   *   *   *

In the neighbourhood of the Weffa-Mosque, in a yard surrounded by the dwellings and huts of poor artisans, there stands an old willow, whose branches are wreathed round by a profusion of climbing roses and wild vines.

In the shadow of this tree a slab of white marble without any inscription covers a grave, at whose head an oil lamp is lit every evening.

The spot ought to be hallowed to every one who respects faithfulness to duty and patriotism, and who has sympathy with the single-hearted hero of a great historic tragedy. The slab covers the remains of the last Greek Emperor, the patriotic and brave Constantine Dragasses.

THE BIBLIOGRAPHY

OF WORKS USED OR CONSULTED FOR THE PRECEDING SKETCH.

I. REPORTS OF THE EYE-WITNESSES OF THE SIEGE.

1. *Annales Georgii Phrantzae Protovestiarii*, printed in *Corpus Scriptorum Historiæ Byzantinae*, Bonnae, 1838.

George Phrantza's father was a chamberlain (Κελλώδης) at the Court of the Emperor Manuel II. Palæologue; his grandfather was the Governor of Prince Constantine, one of the younger sons of that Emperor. George Phrantza and Prince Constantine (who was later to be the *last* Greek Emperor) were educated together; their friendship commenced in their earliest boyhood, and lasted through life. As an able diplomatist Phrantza was often sent as envoy of the Emperor to different courts. Being one of theEmperor's suite, he was personally engaged in the defence of Constantinople. He was made a prisoner by the Turks, but succeeded in paying his ransom and retired to Corfu, where in the year 1462 he entered the Monastery of St Elias, and at the pressing request of the Greek patriots wrote his Memoirs.

2. *Lettera de la presa di Constantinopoli, di Leonardo da Scio, Arcivescovo di Metelino, scritta a Papa Nicolo V.,*

intorna la presa di Constantinopoli, ex Scio, xvi. Augusto 1453.

Archbishop Leonardo came to the Greek capital in November 1452, accompanying Cardinal Isidore, the Legate of the Pope. He was personally engaged in the defence of the city. His report to the Pope is justly considered as most valuable and trustworthy. There exist several editions of his letter. I have used that one printed in the collection of Sansovino, Venice, 1573.

3. *Lettera d'Issidoro Ruteno, Cardinale e Vescovo Sabino, della presa di Constantinopoli, nella quale egli si ritrovo Legate del Papa.* Ed. Sansovino, Venetia, 1573.

At one time a Russian Archbishop, and after the Council of Florence in 1438 one of the staunchest supporters of the union with Rome, he came to Constantinople as the Pope's Legate to accept the formal submission of the Greek Church. During the siege he was, at least nominally, the commander of one of the most important positions at the walls.

4. *Giornale dell' Assedio di Constantinopoli,* 1453, *di Nicolo Barbaro, P.V.,* corredeto di note e documenti per Enrico Cornet, Vienna, 1856.

Barbaro, a Venetian nobleman, was himself in Constantinople when the Turks began the siege, and he joined his compatriots in its defence. He kept a Journal of the most striking events, which enables us to follow the great drama day by day.

5. *Informacion envoyée* par Francesco de Tresves à J. R. père en Dieu, Monseigneur le Cardinal d'Avignon, &c., *par Jehan Blanchin et Jacques Tedardi, Florentin, de l'entreprise de Constantinople, faicte par l'Empereur Turc le 29 jour de Mai l'an 1453, à laquelle le dict Jacques etstoit présent.*

This "Informacion" has been published in *Chroniques*

de Charles VII. roi de France, par T. Chartier, Paris, 1858 (vol. iii. p. 20–25). Tedardi fought on the walls when the Turks entered Constantinople, and had much difficulty in gaining the harbour, where he threw himself into the water to escape Turkish slavery. He was seen and picked up by a Venetian boat. His report abounds with interesting details.

6. *Ubertini Pusculi Brixiensis,* Carmen de capta Constantinopolis libri quatuor.

Ubertino Pusculo, a citizen of Brescia, had been living in Constantinople for some time before the siege, and remained there to the end. He succeeded in escaping from slavery, and wrote a poem describing some incidents of the siege and the capture of the city.

7. Θρῆνος δης Κωνσδαντινοπόπολεως.

This is an elegiac poem describing the siege and the fall of the Capital, with such graphic power and such a minute knowledge of details, that there is no doubt but that the writer took part in the defence, and was in a position to obtain accurate and extensive information. The poet was afraid to publish his name, but indicated certain signs to enable his friends to identify the author.

The Θρῆνος as well as Ubertini Pusculi's poem have been printed in *Analekten der Mittel und Neu-Griechischen Literatur,* von A. Elisser, Leipzig, 1857.

8. *Skazaniya o Vzyatii Tzar-grada bezbojnim turetzkim Saltanom.* ("The Reports of the Capture of Constantinople by the godless Turkish Sultan.") This is a Slavonic manuscript kept in Chilandari, a monastery on Mount Athos, of which several copies exist. After comparing five copies in Russian libraries, Sreznyevsky gave an abstract of them in his essay "Povyest o Tzaregradye," read before

the Imperial Academy of Science at St Petersburg (*Memoirs of the Second Division*, 1854, i. 99–137). His own impression was that some Greeks who had escaped to Russia, related the details of which they were eye-witnesses. But the manuscript is so full of the idioms of the Balkan Slavs, that it is more likely it was written by some Bulgarian or Serbian closely connected with the Court and Greek headquarters. The graphic descriptions of incidents do not permit a doubt of the writer relating what he actually saw happen. In the citations I have called this MS. the "Slavonic Chronicle."

9. *Memoirs of the Janissary Michael Konstantinovich.*

Michael Konstantinovich was a Serbian knight, born at Ostrovitza, taken prisoner by the Turks in 1455, and enrolled amongst the Janissaries. He served in the Sultan's army some years, and then went to Poland, where, about 1490, he wrote his Memoirs. He devoted a chapter to events connected with the siege of Constantinople, giving some interesting details. He was himself with the Serbian contingent in the Turkish camp. His detachment was stationed opposite to the gate of Adrianople, but, as he adds, "*as far as our help went, the Turk would never have taken the city.*"

The MS., written in a peculiar mixture of Serbian and Polish, was first translated into Bohemian, and printed under the title *Historia neb Kronyka Turecka*, Lytomisc, 1565. The original text was published under the title *Pamietniki Janiczara* by Galezowsky in his *Zbior pisarzow Polskieh* (vol. v., p. 128), Warsaw, 1828.

II. Contemporary Writers.

1. *Ducae, Michaeli Ducae nepotis, Historia Byzantina* (ed. Bonnac, 1834).

This writer was a distinguished statesman and Greek patriot, proud of his family connection with the old Imperial dynasty of Ducas. Shortly previous to the siege he was at Constantinople, but apparently left the city before the declaration of war. He conscientiously says that he repeats what he heard from others. Personally he belonged to that minority of intelligent Greeks who were decidedly for the alliance with Western Europe, even at the cost of the submission of the Greek Church to the Pope.

2. *Laonici Chalcochondylae, Turcica historia* (Bonnae, 1834).

Laonic (Nicola) and his brother Demetrius had been intimately connected with the Court of the Prince Demetrius, brother of the unfortunate Emperor Constantin. Laonic had exceptional opportunities of knowing the interior life of both the Greek and Turkish Courts, his brother having been once Prince Demetrius' envoy to the Sultan.

3. *Critobulus, De rebus gestis Mechemetis II. inde ab anno 1451, usque ad annum 1467.* (Printed in Caroli Mulleri, *fragmenta Historicorum Graecorum*, vol. v., Parisiis, 1870.)

"Critobulus of Imbros," a Greek in the Turkish service, was a man of keen intellect and of much literary ability. He dedicated his work to the Conqueror Mohammed II., but in his account of men and events he shows great impartiality.

4. *Tarich Muntechebati Evli Chelebi.*

This Turkish historian lived late in the fifteenth century. Writing of the conquest, he states that *Korosh-Dede*, one of the Turkish heroes of the siege, was a pupil of his own grandfather, *Turkhan Chodja Ahmed Yussuphy*. Dr Mordtmann has given a translation of Chelebi's version, in the Appendix to his own work on the siege.

5. *Zorzi Dolphin, Assedio e presa di Constantinopoli nell anno* 1453, estratto dalla Cronaca delle famiglie nobili di Venezia e della stessa citta dalla sua origine sino l'anno 1478.

Dolphin says that he used not only the written reports of Leonardo of Chios and of Philippo da Rimano, *but also what he heard from those who were eye-witnesses* (pp. 9 and 43). His work was printed by George M. Thomas in the *Sitzungs-Berichte der Kgl. bayerischen Akademie der Wissenschaften*, Munich, 1868.

6. *Theodore Spandugin Cantacuzin*, gentilhuomo Constantinopolitano, J. *Comentari, Del origine e costumi Turchi*, Fiorenza, 1551. Improved edition in C. N. Sathas, *Monumenta Historiæ Hellenicæ*, vol. ix., Paris, 1888.

In his commentaries on Turkish questions, which were much appreciated in Italy in the sixteenth century, Spandugin gave some interesting particulars of the fall of Constantinople. Being one of the family of the Cantacuzens, several members of which fell defending the capital, and having been nearly related to Kyr Lucas Notaras, the Admiral of the Greek fleet, he doubtless wrote down details accepted by his family as facts. I follow him especially in the closing scene.

7. Abraham the Armenian, *Mélodie élégiaque sur la prise de Stamboul*, traduite par M. Brosset (printed in Lebeau's *Histoire du Bas-Empire*, vol. xxi. pp. 307–314). Another translation into French was made by Mr Eugène Boré, and printed in the *Journal Asiatique* for 1835.

The Armenian poet declares in the Introduction that having visited Constantinople "in its glory and admired its holy relics," and having now heard of its fall, he felt moved to put into a poem that which he heard.

8. Georgii Scholarii, Κατα τῆς Σιμονιακῆς αἰρέσεως, ἤτοι ἀπιστίας (Contra Simoniacam hæresiam, sive infidelitatem). Monk Genadius' Memorandum against the union with Rome, printed in J. P. Migne, *Patrologiæ cursus*, vol. clx. pp. 731–8.

III. CONTEMPORARY LETTERS AND OFFICIAL DOCUMENTS.

1. Francisci Philelphi, *Epistolae*, A.D. 1437–1472. Venetiis, 1493. The second edition, Parisiis, 1503.

2. Reusnerii, *Epistolarum Turcicarum*, libri v., printed in Francfort, 1598.

3. Odorici Raynaldi, *Annales Ecclesiastici*, vol. xviii. (containing letters from the year 1417 to 1458). Coloniae Agrippinae, 1694.

4. *Acta Archivi Veneti*, ed. Dr Yanko Schafarik. Belgrade, 1866.

5. *Monumenta (Archivi Veneti) spectantia Slavorum Meridionalium*, edited by the South Slavonic Academy of Science, Agram, 1868.

IV. MODERN WRITERS.

Naturally all the modern works treating the history of the Byzantine Empire or that of the Turkish Empire have special chapters dedicated to the fall of Constantinople. I will mention here only those which are considered as standard works or which are monographs.

1. Gibbon, *Decline and Fall of the Roman Empire* (ch. lxviii., vol. iii.). All the sources from which Gibbon

drew his information were: Phrantza, Ducas, Chalcochondylas, and the letter of the Archbishop of Chios.

2. Joseph v. Hammer, *Geschichte des Osmanischen Reiches*, vol. i. book xii. In addition to the Byzantine and Italian works, Hammer was well acquainted with Sa'ad-ud-din.

3. George Finlay, *A History of Greece*, edited by Rev. H. F. Tozer, Oxford, 1877. The fall of Constantinople is described in the third volume, from p. 496.

4. Zinkeisen, J. W., *Geschichte des Osmanischen Reiches*. The author was able to use some letters and reports found in the Vatican Library.

5. J. Martin et M. Brosset, *Histoire du Bas-Empire par Lebeau*, Paris, 1835. The editors were able to improve Lebeau's description by a few details found in the poem of the Armenian Abraham and in the so-called "Grusian Chronicle."

6. J. Stassulevich, *Ossada i Vzyatiye Vizantii Turkami* (St Petersburg, 1854), consulted only the old Byzantine sources and the Chronicle of Sa'ad-ud-din.

7. Sreznyevski, *Povyest o Tzaregradye*, St Petersburg, 1855.

8. Dr A. D. Mordtmann has given us one of the most interesting descriptions in his *Belagerung und Eroberung Constantinopels durch die Türken im Jahre* 1453, *nach Original quellen bearbeitet* (Stuttgart, 1858), using largely the Journal of Nicolo Barbaro.

9. Dr Y. U. Krause, *Die Eroberungen von Constantinopel im xiii und xiv Jahrhunderte nach Byzantinischen, Frankischen, und Turkischen quellen und Berichten*, Halle, 1870, drew chiefly from Byzantine authors, reprinting some portions

from Sa'ad-ud-din, and taking some incidents from the poem of a Greek eye-witness.

10. Rev. W. J. Broadribb and Mr Walter Besant, *Constantinople : a Sketch of its History from its Foundation to its Conquest by the Turks in 1453*, London, 1879, followed Mordtmann and Krause, but consulted also independently Byzantine authors, and added some interesting information on the condition of Constantinople from the French knight, Bertrandon de la Brocquière.

11. The latest monograph in Western literature is that written by E. H. Vlasto, *Les derniers jours de Constantinople*, Paris, 1883.

Mr Vlasto's bibliography mentions as the principal works in modern Greek which treat of this subject:—

    S. D. Byzantios, *Constantinople*.
    Spir. Zambelios, *Byzantine Essays*.
    Marc Renieri, *Historical Essays*.
    S. N. Sathas, *Historical Works*.
    Const. Paparrigopoulo, *The General History of the Hellenic Nations*, &c.

www.ingramcontent.com/pod-product-compliance
Lightning Source LLC
Chambersburg PA
CBHW032147230426
43672CB00011B/2481